The Healthy BREAKS COOKBOOK

Compiled by
Catherine Beattie

DISCOVERY BOOKS

Discovery Books

29 Hacketts Lane, Pyrford, Woking, Surrey GU22 8PP

Acknowledgements

My warmest thanks to all the talented chefs and the health resorts for their recipes: Michael Welch at *Cedar Falls*, Adam Palmer at *Champneys*, Jean Alexander at *Forest Mere*, Simon Gurney at *Grayshott Hall*, Trevor Hancock at *Henlow Grange*, Richard Greenough at *Hoar Cross Hall*, Mark Scudder at *Inglewood*, Paul Spink at *Ragdale Hall*, Robert Coppin at *Shrubland Hall*, John Harvey at *Springs Hydro* and Teresa and Mac Browning at *Stobo Castle*.

Some recipes have been reproduced with kind permission from other publications - *The Inglewood Way to Health* published by David and Charles, *The Champneys Cookbook* published by Boxtree and the recipe books of *Henlow Grange/Springs Hydro, Shrubland Hall* and *Ragdale Hall*.

I am also grateful to David Simpson for his invaluable help with all aspects of production. In addition to his considerable design and typesetting skills, David has also drawn all the delightful food illustrations used on the recipe pages.

Finally my love and thanks to Alec and the family for their encouragement, support and inspiration - Julie, Stefan and little Josh, Clare and John, Kevin, Sarah, Alison, Jonathan, Thomas and Stephen - and my dear mother, Winifred Hunt.

Production and illustrations by David Simpson

Printed and bound in Hong Kong

British Library Cataloguing in Publication Data

A catalogue record for this book is available from the British Library

ISBN 0 951851 6 0

CONTENTS

Measurement Tips

All the recipes used in this book are selected from the menus of the credited health resorts. To avoid confusion, it has been necessary to slightly modify the metric measurements supplied in some recipes, so all dishes have the same imperial to metric conversions.

Approximate conversion tables

Volume		Weights	
1 fl oz	35ml	1/2oz	15g
2	70	3/4	20
2 1/2	90	1	30
3	105	1 1/2	45
4	150	2	55
5	175	2 1/2	70
6	200	3	85
8	285	4	115
10	330	4 1/2	130
12	425	5	140
16	570	6	170
20	700	7	200
1 1/2 pints	900	8	225
28	1 litre	9	225
2 pints	1.12 litres	10	285
		1lb	450
		2	910
		3	1kg 350g

Oven temperatures

Mark 1	275°F	140°C
2	300	150
3	325	170
4	350	180
5	375	190
6	400	200
7	425	220
8	450	230
9	475	240

1 level teaspoon = 5ml
1 level tablespoon = 15ml
1 level dessertspoon = 10ml

All eggs used are medium size 3 unless otherwise stated

Introduction

Delicious, low calorie cuisine is one of the highlights of staying at any of the health resorts featured in this book. While the menus reflect the character and style of the individual resorts, the food served is relatively simple, prepared from fresh ingredients, cooked with care and well presented. Appetites are pampered with home-made soups and breads, colourful salads, fresh vegetables, choice meat, fish, pasta and vegetarian dishes, fruit and even low calorie desserts. Whether you opt for Champneys' healthy haute cuisine, Shrubland Hall's famous 'Rohkost' vegetarian diet or the appetising fare served at any of the other resorts - the aim is to revitalise your taste buds while rejuvenating your body!

You may be surprised to find the culinary emphasis is no longer on diets, fasting or even calorie counting anymore, but on achieving optimum health through sensible nutrition. Food is carefully chosen for its nutritional quality, variety and taste. Moderation not deprivation, is the key to achieving good lifelong eating habits and a balanced diet means enjoying most foods occasionally, even puddings and special treats.

Of course, if you *do* want to lose weight, you'll be given every help and encouragement. Dietary advice may be offered at your initial consultation or arranged on request. Menus are helpfully calorie counted or colour coded so you can keep an eye on your daily intake. Some health resorts have special 'light' dining areas to help slimmers resist the temptations of the main dining room!

All the recipes in this book have been selected from the regular menus of eleven of Britain's top health resorts - *Cedar Falls, Champneys, Forest Mere, Grayshott Hall, Henlow Grange, Hoar Cross Hall, Inglewood, Ragdale Hall, Shrubland Hall, Springs Hydro* and *Stobo Castle*. If you've had the pleasure of staying at any of these establishments, you may well recognise some of your favourite dishes. With a few exceptions, all recipes were chosen for their simplicity and are easily prepared from everyday ingredients. I hope you enjoy them and wish you good health and bon appetit!

Catherine Beattie
April 1995

Health Resorts Featured

CEDAR FALLS HEALTH FARM
Bishop Lydeard Taunton Somerset TA4 3HR
Tel 01823 433233 Fax 01823 432777
A popular health farm situated on a 44
acre estate close to the Exmoor National
Park. Cedar Falls boasts extensive leisure
facilities with indoor and outdoor pools,
trout fishing and golf. The emphasis here
is on relaxation with visitors offered stress

management workshops as well as a full range of body and beauty treatments.
Catering manager Michael Welch creates and cooks the appetising menus served in
the main and 'light' dining rooms. Wine served.

Recipes

Cream of Celery Soup	*Meatballs in Rich Mushroom Sauce*
Oriental Soup	*Kiwi Cheesecake*

CHAMPNEYS HEALTH RESORT
Wiggington Tring Hertfordshire HP23 6HY
Tel 01442 863351 Fax 01442 872342
As Britain's most famous health
resort, Champneys offers a unique
ambience and an outstanding range of
treatments and facilities. The
exquisitely prepared food is on a par

with the best offered in five star hotels, and is served in two attractive dining
rooms. Head chef Adam Palmer's wonderful haute cuisine recipes appeal to
the eye as well as the taste buds. Wine served.

Recipes

Avocado and Sweetcorn Soup	*Celeriac and Wild Mushroom Terrine*
Carrot, Scallop and Corriander Soup	*Red Mullet and Salad Nicoise*
Chick Pea, Olive and Garlic Soup	*Banana en Papillote*
Mexican Bean Soup	*Ice Cream*
Summer Gazpacho	*Lemon and Orange Chiffon Pie*
Chicken Breast Stuffed with Carrots,	
* Leeks and Black Olives*	

FOREST MERE

Liphook Hampshire GU30 7JQ
Tel 01428 722051   Fax 01428 723501
Peacefully situated overlooking a picturesque
lake, Forest Mere offers expert guidance
and support in improving diet and lifestyle.
A full range of exercise classes and leisure
activities is available. Treatment areas have been refurbished with comfortable changing
facilities, pristine therapy rooms, hydrotherapy baths, power showers and a splendid
new sauna. Forest Mere's innovative chef, Jean Alexander, has introduced exciting new
pasta recipes into the menus served in the two dining rooms. No alcohol served.

Recipes

Strawberry and Melon Starter

Cold Cucumber and Mint Soup

Lettuce and Courgette Soup

Sweetcorn and Coriander Soup

Baby Chicken with Mint and Pineapple

Lasagnette with Chicken, Mango and Raisins

Orange Roast Lamb

Salmon and Herb Loaf

Sole Fillets with Prawns, Grapes and Asparagus

Tagliolini with Prawns and Radicchio

Broccoli and Tomato Pasta

Leek and Gruyere Pasta

Pasta with Broad Beans and Grainy Mustard

Spinach and Cottage Cheese Pasta

Nectarine Sorbet

Forest Mere Cake

GRAYSHOTT HALL
HEALTH FITNESS RETREAT

Grayshott Near Hindhead Surrey GU26 6JJ
Tel 01428 604331   Fax 01428 605463
Grayshott Hall is set in lovely National Trust
countryside and offers an excellent range of
treatments, classes and leisure facilities,
including indoor tennis courts and a 9-hole golf course. Head chef Simon Gurney uses fresh
herbs and quality ingredients in his simply prepared and satisfying menus served in two
pleasant dining rooms. No alcohol served except on special occasions like Christmas Day.

Recipes

Melon, Prawn and Raspberry Cocktail

Prosciutto with Tropical Fruit

Cream of Mushroom Soup

Chicken Supreme with Orange and Lemon

Sirloin Steak with Tarragon and Mustard Sauce

Creole Cod Fillet

Haddock Fillets with Coriander and Orange

Apricot Roulade with Raspberries

Lemon and Honey Syllabub with Strawberries

Pineapple and Strawberry Strudel

Summer Pudding

Henlow Grange Health Farm

Henlow Bedfordshire SG16 6DP

Tel 01462 811111   Fax 01462 815310

Situated in Bedfordshire countryside, Henlow Grange is Britain's largest health resort and with a huge range of treatments and leisure faciities. Day guest programmes are particularly popular and good value. The extensive and varied menu created by head chef Trevor Hancock include low calorie but substantial starters, main courses and salads plus some very tasty puddings. Wine served.

Recipes

Avocado Salad with Beansprouts

Melon and Cucumber Refresher

Smoked Trout Tomatoes

Curried Parsnip Soup

Lemon and Spring Onion Soup

Orange and Carrot Soup

Tomato and Basil Soup

Sole Fillets with Red Pepper Sauce

Chinese Stir Fry

Fillet Steak Medallions with Peppercorns

Vegetable and Aubergine Galette

Vegetable Korma

Vegetable Pizza

Fresh Fruit Brulee

St Clements Mousse

Carrot Cake

Hoar Cross Hall Health Spa Resort

Hoar Cross Nr Yoxall Staffordshire DE13 8QS

Tel 01283 575671   Fax 01283 575652

Hidden away in the heart of rural Staffordshire, Hoar Cross Hall opened in 1991 and was the first health resort to offer a complete range of continental thalassotherapy treatments. The striking stately home has been lovingly transformed into a luxurious health resort and offers exceptional accommodation, treatments and cuisine. Head chef Richard Greenough's delicous menus use fresh ingredients and an abundance of fruit and vegetables - served in two attractive restaurants by friendly staff. Wine served.

Recipes

Citrus Savoury Salad

Fan of Melon served on a Fresh Mint Coulis

Parsnip Heart of the Country Soup

Breast of Chicken Coq au Leekie

Medallions of Monkfish au Poivre

Apple and Almond Mousse

Raspberry and Mango Flan

INGLEWOOD HEALTH HYDRO

Kintbury Berkshire RG15 0SW

Tel 01488 682022 Fax 01488 682595

Standing in 40 acres of parkland, Inglewood Health Hydro offers a generous number of daily inclusive treatments carried out by a caring staff. Expert dietary advice is given and slimmers can eat their meals in the pleasant 'light' dining room. An appetising choice of menus is offered, many using vegetables and salads from Inglewood's own gardens, carefully prepared and cooked by head chef Mark Scudder and his team. Wine served.

Recipes

Artichoke with Broad Beans

Avocado and Grapefruit

Crab and Mango Salad

Crabmeat in Foil Parcels

Mozzarella and Tomato Salad

Cream of Watercress Soup

Mushroom and Tarragon Soup

Potato, Onion and Celery Soup

Chicken Pilaf

Lamb and Rice with Apricots

Mustard Rabbit

Baked Herring with Tomatoes

Malaysian Fish Curry

Artichoke with Broad Beans

Baked Green Omelette

Mozzarella, Watercress and Orange Salad

Mushroom Souffle

Apple Souffle

Rhubarb Meringue

Special Pineapple Surprise

RAGDALE HALL HEALTH HYDRO

Ragdale Nr Melton Mowbray Leic. LE14 3PB

Tel 01664 434831 Fax 01664 434587

One of Britain's most luxurious health resorts, Ragdale Hall has excellent leisure facilities and a superb range of beauty treatments and therapies. A friendly health resort - guests share long tables in the dining room where head chef Paul Spink's wholesome and appetising food is enjoyed -generous hot and cold lunch buffets and satisfying dinner menus. Wine served.

Recipes

Atholl Brose

Baby Pineapple brimming with Exotic Fruits

Ragout of Summer Fruits

Yoghurt Refresher

Chilled Beetroot and Orange Soup

Smoked Haddock Soup

Spinach and Blue Cheese Soup

Fillet of Beef with an Oatmeal Crust

Noisette of Lamb with Reform Sauce

Supreme of Chicken with Passion Fruit Sauce

Baked Trout with a Hazelnut and Lemon Sauce

Root Vegetable Ragout

Wholemeal Pancakes with a Fruit Filling

Bacon and Herb Scones

SHRUBLAND HALL HEALTH CLINIC

Coddenham Nr Ipswich Suffolk IP6 9QH
Tel 01473 830404 Fax 01473 832641
This is a unique health resort run on
serious nature cure lines under the
supervision of doctors and nurses.
The atmosphere, nonetheless, is friendly and welcoming and many 'patients'
return regularly year after year for its special ambience and cuisine. Shrubland
Hall serves only vegetarian raw food meals which can be adapted to suit
most needs. Chef Robert Coppin masterminds the imaginative assortment of
'Rohkost' menus which include exotic salads, raw fruit, vegetable soups and
broths, home-made yoghurt and wholegrain bread, baked from wheat and
barley grown on the Shrubland Hall Estate.

Recipes

Mixed Vegetable Soup

Apricot and Almond Salad

Avocado Salad

Slimmer's Pineapple Special

Apple and Cheese Tea Bread

Honey and Orange Bran Bread

SPRINGS HYDRO

Packington Nr Ashby de la Zouch
Leicestershire LE6 5ITG
Tel 01530 273873 Fax 01530 270987
Springs is Britain's first purpose built
health resort and opened in August
1990. It successfully combines the
convenience and comfort of modern

accommodation with an extensive array of amenities, treatments and exercise
facilities. John Harvey is Springs' innovative chef who prepares a delicious
assortment of healthy menus to satisfy the most discerning visitor.

Recipes

Savoury Pancakes

Hot Spiced Pork in Mustard Sauce

Turkey Roulade with Cranberry Sauce

Steamed Mackerel with Tomato
    and Black Olive Sauce

Steamed Smoked Salmon
    with Spinach and Nutmeg Sauce

Cauliflower and Pasta Bake

Light Nut Roast

Baked Apples
    with Cinnamon Fromage Frais

Plum and Orange Cobbler

Apricot and Prune Loaf

STOBO CASTLE HEALTH SPA

Stobo Castle Peebleshire EG45 8NY

Tel 01721 760249 Fax 01721 760294

Stobo Castle is the perfect health
retreat, situated in glorious isolation
amid beautiful Scottish scenery. The
atmosphere is warm and informal with
log fires, cosy and luxurious rooms and a

generous programme of inclusive treatments and therapies. Stobo's chef is Teresa
Browning who serves up simple Scottish fare cooked to perfection with the
minimum of calories and fat. The soups and low calorie desserts are irresistible -
you'll find yourself asking for seconds!

Recipes

Broccoli and Chive Soup

Carrot and Parsley Soup

Celery and Apple Soup

Minestrone Soup

Watercress and Potato Soup

Fillet of Pink Trout
  with Watercress Puree

Stir Fry Vegetables with Noodles

Vegetarian Haggis
  with Neeps and Tatties

Baked Egg Custard
  with Fresh Rhubarb

Baked Pineapple with Meringue

Creme Reverse

Fresh Fruit Compote

Raspberry Fool

Strawberry and Melon Starter, Forest Mere

Atholl Brose

RAGDALE HALL

A delicious breakfast dish that can be prepared in advance.
160 kcals per portion • Serves 4

2oz/55g medium oatmeal	8fl oz/285ml low fat natural yoghurt
5oz/140g raspberries	3fl oz/105 ml Greek yoghurt
3 teaspoons clear honey	

Spread out the oatmeal in a grill pan and toast lightly until golden brown (be careful not to burn). When cool, combine honey and yoghurts in a large bowl and whisk until stiffened. Carefully fold in most of the oatmeal and 4oz/115g of the raspberries. Serve chilled in individual bowls garnished with the remaining raspberries and oatmeal.

Avocado and Grapefruit

INGLEWOOD

120 kcals per portion • Serves 4

2 large grapefruit	I lettuce
I avocado	

Peel the grapefruit removing all pith and cut into thin slices, pouring any juice into a bowl. Peel the avocado and cut into slivers. Sprinkle with the grapefruit juice and mix with the grapefruit slices. Lay the lettuce in a serving dish, and arrange the slices of grapefruit and avocado on top. If extra dressing is needed, sprinkle lettuce with a little lemon juice or French dressing.

Avocado Salad with Beansprouts

HENLOW GRANGE

229 kcals per portion • Serves 4

1 ripe avocado	2oz/55g sweetcorn kernels
juice and zest of a lemon	1oz/30g button mushrooms, sliced
4oz/115g beansprouts	2oz/55g hazelnuts, toasted and chopped

Peel, stone and dice the avocado. Place in a large bowl with the lemon juice and zest. Carefully fold in the beansprouts, sweetcorn and mushrooms, taking care not to break up the avocado. Divide between 4 plates and sprinkle over with the toasted hazelnuts. Serve chilled. *(Substituting the hazelnuts with fresh chopped herbs saves 80 kcals per serving.)*

Baby Pineapple brimming with Exotic Fruits

RAGDALE HALL

75 kcals per portion • Serves 4

2 baby pineapples	1 small star fruit
2 kiwi fruit	8 strawberries
8 lychees	1/2 papaya or paw paw

Cut the pineapples in half lengthways and cut out the flesh to leave an empty shell. Skin and de-stone the remaining fruit where necessary and cut into cubes. Mix the fruits together and pile into the empty pineapple shells. Finish off with a splash of kirsch if desired.

Citrus Savoury Salad

HOAR CROSS HALL

kcals 220 • Serves 2

1 large orange	1 teaspoon lemon juice
1/2 red dessert apple	1 teaspoon vegetable oil
1 celery heart	1 teaspoon soft brown sugar
1oz/30g seedless raisins	1/2 lettuce
1 teaspoon orange juice	

Peel and dice the orange, dice the apple, mix both with the chopped celery and raisins. Make the dressing from the orange and lemon juice, oil and sugar. Arrange the fruit mixture on a bed of lettuce leaves and sprinkle with the dressing, or serve in the orange shell with the lettuce surround.

Crab and Mango Salad

INGLEFIELD HEALTH HYDRO

This unusual starter comes from the West Indies, where crabs and mangoes are plentiful and cheap.

75 kcals per portion • Serves 4

6oz/170g white crabmeat

1 large mango

juice of ½ lemon

lettuce leaves

salt and freshly ground black pepper

Flake the crabmeat and sprinkle with the lemon juice. Peel the mango and cut into thin slices. Mix with the crabmeat and serve on a bed of lettuce leaves. Season with salt and freshly ground black pepper.

Crabmeat in Foil Parcels

INGLEWOOD HEALTH HYDRO

93 kcals per portion • Serves 4

6oz/170g crabmeat, canned or fresh

8oz/225g flat mushrooms

1 aubergine

4 tablespoons dry sherry (fino)

salt and pepper

Clean the vegetables, removing the hard base of the aubergine and any hard stems of the mushrooms. Cut the aubergine into thin vertical slices, sprinkle with salt and allow to stand for at least 30 minutes. Drain off the bitter juices, and wipe the aubergine pieces. Finely chop the mushrooms. Take four squares of foil and place a slice of aubergine, mushrooms and crabmeat on each piece. Grind on a little pepper and sprinkle 1 tablespoon of sherry onto each package. Fold each package carefully allowing no liquid to escape and bake in a medium oven (350°F 180°C. Gas Mark 4) for 15 to 20 minutes. Serve in the foil packets. A dish of simple boiled rice is the traditional accompaniment - but mashed potatoes go well too.

Fan of Melon served on a Fresh Mint Coulis

HOAR CROSS HALL

kcals 55 • serves 4

1 honeydew melon	strawberries for garnish
1 bunch of fresh mint	small pot of natural yoghurt
5 fl oz/175ml mango puree	splash of sparkling wine *(optional)*

Peel the melon, remove seeds and cut into eight boat-shaped portions (allow two pieces per serving). Finely chop half the mint leaving a few nice sprigs for garnish. Add yoghurt, puree, wine and chopped mint together to make the mint sauce and divide between the four plates. Chop up 4 potions of melon and make four piles on top of the sauce on each plate. Fan out the remaining melon pieces and place against the plated melon keeping the fan upright. Slice four strawberries and fan out one on each plate. Garnish with sprig of fresh mint.

Melon, Prawn and Raspberry Cocktail

GRAYSHOTT HALL

85 kcals per portion • Serves 4

1 large galia or charentais melon	6oz/170g fresh raspberries
8oz/225g peeled prawns	4 sprigs of mint

Peel, seed and dice the melon and gently combine with the prawns and raspberries. Chill for 1 hour. Serve in glass dishes garnished with mint.

Melon and Cucumber Refresher

HENLOW GRANGE

18 kcals per portion • Serves 4

1 ripe cantaloupe or honeydew melon	1 tablespoon mint leaves freshly chopped
½ cucumber diced	- leave some for garnishing

Halve and de-seed the melon. Using a parisienne cutter, scoop out some melon balls. Alternatively cut the melon into wedges, slice away the skin and cube the flesh. Fold all the ingredients together, cover and chill for at least 2 hours. Serve very cold, garnished with a sprig of mint.

Mozzarella and Tomato Salad
INGLEWOOD HEALTH HYDRO

*A delicious starter with a decidedly Italian flavour -
tastes great served outdoors on a warm summer day..*
138 kcals per portion • Serves 4

1lb/450g tomatoes	1 tablespoon fresh basil, shredded
4oz/115g mozzarella cheese	1 tablespoon olive oil
1 small onion	

Cut the mozzarella into thin slices. Slice the tomatoes thinly horizontally and cut the onion into thin rings. Spread the ingredients on a plate and sprinkle with the olive oil and basil. Serve with crispbread or melba toast.

Prosciutto with Tropical Fruit
GRAYSHOTT HALL

110 kcals per portion • Serves 4

8 very thick slices of Parma ham	4 figs
1/2 papaya, peeled and seeded	4 strawberries, halved
1/2 galia melon, made into melon balls	4 leaves Lollo Rosso lettuce

Place the lettuce on plates. Arrange ham on plates and surround with halved strawberries, figs, sliced papaya and melon balls.

Ragoût of Summer Fruits
RAGDALE HALL

Make the most of plentiful supplies of summer fruits with this refreshing starter
65 kcals per portion • Serves 4

5oz/140g loganberries	4 teaspoons low calorie sweetener
5oz/140g raspberries	1 vanilla pod
5oz/140g blackcurrants	4 tablespoons Greek yoghurt
5oz/140g strawberries	2fl oz/70ml low sugar blackcurrant cordial
juice of 1/2 lemon	

Put all ingredients, except the yoghurt, into a saucepan with a tablespoon of water. Stir gently over a very low heat until the sweetener has dissolved. Remove the vanilla pod and chill the mixture for 2 to 4 hours (or overnight). Serve in 4 separate ramekin dishes topped with a tablespoon of yoghurt. Tinned or frozen fruits may be substituted but do not give as good a result.

Savoury Pancakes

SPRINGS HYDRO

131 kcals per portion • Serves 4

¹/₂ pint/285ml skimmed milk	1 large tomato, de-seeded and diced
1¹/₂oz/45g plain flour	2 tablespoons low fat natural yoghurt
1 egg	1 tablespoon fresh parsley, chopped
4oz/115g smoked chicken (or ham or tuna fish)	ground black pepper

Make the pancakes by beating together milk, flour and egg until smooth. Rub a drop of oil over the base of a 8inch/20.5cm frying pan. Allow the base of the pan to get very hot before pouring in some of the batter. Cook until golden brown. Transfer to a plate and leave to cool. Continue cooking the remaining pancakes. Mix together the smoked chicken, tomato, yoghurt and parsley. Season to taste with freshly ground black pepper. Divide between the 4 cold pancakes and roll up into cigar shapes. Serve whole or sliced, garnished with fresh herbs or salad leaves.

Smoked Trout Tomatoes

HENLOW GRANGE

95 kcals per portion • Serves 4

6oz/170g smoked trout fillets	2 tablespoons natural yoghurt
juice of ¹/₂ lemon	ground black pepper
1 tablespoon chopped parsley	4 large firm tomatoes

Remove any visible bones on the trout fillets. Place trout, lemon juice and parsley in a food processor or liquidiser and process until smooth. Add the yoghurt and quickly blend in. Season to taste with freshly ground black pepper. Transfer the mixture to a bowl, cover and chill until required. Slice the top off each tomato and carefully scoop out the flesh. Make sure the tomatoes sit firmly on their base. Spoon the trout mixture into each tomato. Serve, garnished with parsley and accompanied with warm pitta bread or toast (adds a further 60/80 calories).

Strawberry and Melon Starter

FOREST MERE

20 kcals per portion • Serves 2

1 small/medium galia or charentais melon   sprig of mint and grapes for garnish
4oz/115g strawberries, sliced

Cut the melon into two generous sized portions and scoop out the seeds. Fill the hollow with the sliced strawberries. Garnish with sliced grapes and mint leaves. Chill for about 30 minutes before serving.

Yoghurt Refresher

RAGDALE HALL

65 kcals per portion • Serves 4

4oz/115g hulled strawberries   12oz/340g low fat natural yoghurt
4fl oz/150ml orange juice

Place all ingredients in a blender for 20 seconds. Put in the fridge and chill well. Serve in wine glasses garnished with finely grated orange rind. This is also delicious with other soft fruits.

Carrot, Scallop and Coriander Soup (top) Chickpea, Olive and Garlic Soup, Champneys

Avocado and Sweetcorn Soup

CHAMPNEYS

88 kcals per portion • Serves 8

1 small onion, finely chopped	20fl oz/700ml chicken stock
1 clove garlic, diced	1 tablespoon natural, low fat fromage frais
7oz/200g sweetcorn kernels, frozen or canned	juice of ½ lemon
2 green over-ripe avocados, peeled and stoned	sea salt and cayenne pepper
1 tablespoon light soy sauce	

Sweat the onion, garlic and about 140g/5oz of sweetcorn in a non-stick pan until the onion is translucent. Mash avocados and add to the pan with soy sauce and chicken stock. Bring to the boil and simmer, uncovered for 20 minutes. Remove from heat and blend the soup in a food processor or blender. Pass through a sieve into a clean pan. Add remaining sweetcorn, bring to the boil, then remove from heat. Stir in fromage frais and lemon juice, and season to taste with salt and cayenne pepper. Serve immediately with warm wholemeal bread.

Broccoli and Chive Soup

STOBO CASTLE

55 kcals per portion • Serves 4

8oz/225g broccoli	20oz/700ml vegetable stock
1 onion	salt and pepper
bunch of chives chopped	

Cook broccoli and onion in vegetable stock until soft. Liquidise and add chives. Bring back to boil for a few seconds and season well. Garnish with a few chopped chives and serve immediately.

Carrot and Parsley Soup

STOBO CASTLE

65 kcals per portion • Serves 4

1lb/450g carrots	small bunch of parsley, chopped
1 onion	salt and pepper
1 pint/570ml vegetable stock	

Prepare the vegetables and boil in vegetable stock until soft. Liquidise in a blender or food processor and add a generous pinch of parsley. Return to the boil and season well. Sprinkle with chopped parsley and serve immediately.

Carrot, Scallop and Coriander Soup

CHAMPNEYS

This haute cuisine soup makes an ideal starter
for a formal dinner party.
Allow time for preparing the scallops.
175 kcals per portion • Serves 4

8 large king scallops	2 teaspoons coriander seeds, crushed
1 dessertspoon virgin olive oil	1oz/30g red lentils
6 medium carrots, chopped	1 bay leaf
1 large onion, chopped	$1^3/_4$ pints/1 litre fish or vegetable stock
1/4 stick celery, chopped	1 bunch fresh coriander
1/2 clove garlic, diced	sea salt and freshly milled black pepper

Remove the scallops from the shells, cutting away any membrane and dark intestines, including the small curved muscle from the white meat. Wash and dry on kitchen paper. Heat the oil in a heavy-based saucepan, then sweat the carrots, onion, celery, garlic and crushed coriander until the onion is transparent. Carefully pick over the lentils to remove any stones before adding to the mixutre with the bay leaf and 4 scallops, each one sliced into thirds. Pour over the stock and bring to the boil; cover the pan, reduce the heat and simmer for 10 minutes. Cut the stalks from the coriander (keep the leaves for garnishing), add to the pan and simmer, covered, for a further 10 minutes. Remove the soup from the heat and allow to cool slightly. Liquidise the soup in a liquidiser or food processor, then pass through a fine sieve. Season with sea salt and freshly milled black pepper to taste. Gently reheat the soup. Fry the remaining 4 scallops in a hot non-stick frying pan for 30 seconds on each side. Place a scallop in the centre of each soup bowl, pour over the soup and garnish with coriander leaves. Serve immediately.

Celery and Apple Soup

STOBO CASTLE

65 kcals per portion • Serves 6

2 heads of celery	2 pints/1.12 litres vegetable stock
1 large Bramley apple	1oz/ 30g Flora margarine
1 medium onion	1oz/30g plain flour
1 small leek	

Thinly slice the celery across the grain and finely chop the onion and leek. Sweat the onion, leek and celery in the margarine in a pan. Add the flour and cook for about 3 minutes. Boil up the vegetable stock and add the ingredients. Peel, core and dice the apple and add to the soup. Simmer for 35 minutes then liquidise. Serve immediately.

Chickpea, Olive and Garlic Soup

CHAMPNEYS

194 kcals per portion • Serves 4

6oz/170g chickpeas	1 bay leaf
1 large onion, finely chopped	1 sprig thyme
1/2 stick celery, finely chopped	2fl oz/70ml extra vigin olive oil
4 large cloves garlic, diced	15 black olives, stoned and diced
28fl oz/1 litre vegetable stock	sea salt and freshly milled white pepper

Soak the chickpeas overnight; then cover with fresh water in a pan and bring to a rapid boil. Simmer for about an hour until tender. Leave to cool, drain and remove outer husks by rubbing them with a cloth. Sweat the chopped onion, celery and garlic until soft in a covered pan. Add the stock, chickpeas, bay leaf and thyme and simmer for 10 minutes. Blend the soup well, slowly adding the olive oil, in a food processor or blender, then pass through a course sieve. Add the black olives as a garnish to finish the soup.

Chilled Beetroot and Orange Soup

RAGDALE HALL

90 kcals per portion • Serves 4

20fl oz/700ml orange juice	8 teaspoons Worcestershire sauce
4fl oz/150ml tomato juice	1 teaspoon fresh basil
8oz/225g cooked beetroot	4 teaspoons low fat natural yoghurt

Place beetroot in a blender for 30 seconds and add remaining ingredients. Liquidise for one minute. Season to taste and refrigerate for 2 to 4 hours until well chilled. Serve in chilled bowls and finish off with a swirl of yoghurt.

Cold Cucumber and Mint Soup

FOREST MERE

70 kcals per portion • Serves 4

1 large cucumber	2 tablespoons cider vinegar
6fl oz/170ml natural yoghurt	2 tablespoons chopped mint
1/2 pint single or non-dairy cream	1 tablespoon chopped tarragon
1 clove garlic	salt and pepper

Wash the cucumber and dry. Grate on a coarse grater into a mixing bowl. Stir in the cream and yoghurt. Peel and crush the garlic and add to the cucumber followed by the vinegar. Season to taste and add the chopped mint and tarragon. Chill well. Serve in individual portions garnished with herbs and shrimps or prawns if desired.

Cream of Celery Soup

CEDAR FALLS HEALTH FARM

50 kcals per portion • Serves 4

8 small sticks celery thinly sliced	2 tablespoons light sour cream
1 large onion finely chopped	2 teaspoons grated Parmesan cheese
20 fl oz/700mls vegetable stock	1 tablespoon chopped parsley
2 tablespoons plain flour	1 teaspoon lemon juice

Combine the celery and onion in half the vegetable stock and cook gently until the celery is tender. Put in the blender for a minute. Return to saucepan and add remaining stock. Mix flour with a little water and add to celery and onion mixture. When the mixture thickens reduce heat and add sour cream, cheese, parsley and lemon juice. Stir well and serve immediately.

Cream of Mushroom Soup

GRAYSHOTT HALL

80 kcals per portion • Serves 4

1 tablespoon vegetable oil	4oz/115g onion, leek and celery, chopped
2 pints/1.12 litres chicken stock	4oz/115g peeled, diced potato
1/4 pint/150ml semi-skimmed milk	bouquet garni
6oz/170g mushrooms	salt and pepper

Wipe and roughly chop the mushrooms. Gently fry the onion, leek and celery until soft. Cool slightly before adding the chicken stock. Stir to the boil. Add the finely diced potato, chopped mushrooms and bouquet garni. Simmmer for 30 minutes. Remove the bouquet garni and liquidise the soup. Add the milk and adjust the seasoning before serving.

Cream of Watercress Soup
INGLEWOOD HEALTH HYDRO
83 kcals per portion • Serves 6

5 bunches of watercress	1 tablespoon chives
12oz/340g potatoes	1 x 16oz/450g carton natural yoghurt
2 medium onions	salt and freshly ground black pepper

Clean the watercress and chop roughly, keeping about 1 tablespoon aside for decoration. Peel the potatoes and onions and cook with the watercress until potatoes are soft. Blend or put through a mouli and allow to cool thorougly. Finely chop the chives and mix these with the yoghurt. Add the watercress and potato mixture a little at a time, mixing well together. Season well with salt and freshly ground black pepper. Decorate with remaining watercress leaves and chill in refrigerator.

Curried Parsnip Soup
HENLOW GRANGE
100 kcals per portion • Serves 4

1lb/450g parsnips, chopped	1 teaspoon mild curry powder
1 large onion, chopped	(or 2 teaspoons curry paste)
1½ pints/900ml chicken stock	fresh herbs to garnish

Place the parsnips, onion, curry powder and stock in a large saucepan. Gradually bring to the boil then cover and simmer for 20 minutes until the parsnips are tender. Puree in a food processor, return to the pan and reheat. Divide the soup between 4 individual warmed bowls, sprinkle with fresh chopped herbs and serve.

Lemon and Spring Onion Soup
HENLOW GRANGE
40 kcals per portion • Serves 6

2 onions, chopped	1 pint/570ml chicken stock
3 sticks of celery, chopped	½ pint/285ml skimmed milk
1 bulb fennel, chopped	4oz/115g spring onions trimmed and chopped
3 lemons	ground black pepper

'Dry fry' vegetables in a large pan with the lid on for 2 to 3 minutes. Peel the rind of lemons and blanch in boiling water. Add this rind and the juice of 2 lemons to pan. Pour on the stock. Bring to the boil, then cover and simmer for 15 to 20 minutes until vegetables are tender. Liquidise soup and return to the pan. Add the milk and spring onions and bring back to the boil. Season to taste and serve hot, garnished with a little chopped spring onion.

Lettuce and Courgette Soup

FOREST MERE

60 kcals per portion • Serves 4

12oz/340g courgettes, grated	2oz/55g cooked potatoes
1/2 iceberg lettuce, shredded	2 tablespoons chervil, chopped
1 1/2 pints/900ml stock	3oz/85ml whipping or non-dairy cream
8oz/225g onions	lemon juice to taste
1 clove garlic	salt and pepper
1/2oz/15g butter	

Melt the butter, add the chopped onion and crushed garlic and cook for five minutes. Add grated courgettes, potato and shredded lettuce. Stir well, add the stock and cook for a further ten minutes. Liquidise, return to a clean pan and reheat slowly. Do not boil. Check the seasoning and correct flavour by adding a little lemon juice. Add the cream just before serving.

Mexican Bean Soup

CHAMPNEYS

The kidney and butter beans must be soaked overnight.
If time is short, tinned pre-soaked beans give a satisfactory result.
156 kcals per portion • Serves 4

3oz/85g dried kidney beans, soaked overnight	1 small red chilli, de-seeded
2oz/55g dried butter beans, soaked overnight	1 teaspoon fresh ginger, peeled and roughly chopped
4 large tomatoes, chopped	1 1/2 pints/900ml water
2 celery sticks, chopped	5fl oz/150ml tomato juice
1 medium onion, chopped	2 teaspoons paprika
1 clove garlic, finely chopped	1 tablespoon fresh parsley, chopped

Bring a pan of water to the boil and add the kidney beans. Bring to the boil again for at least 10 minutes. At the same time, boil another pan of water and add the butter beans and cook in the same way. Drain the beans and place in a pan with the vegetables and all the other ingredients except for the tomato juice, paprika and parsley. Cover and simmer for 1 1/2 hours until the beans are tender. Remove the chilli pepper and liquidise the soup in a food processor or blender and then pass through a fine sieve. Pour in the tomato juice and reheat gently. Season to taste. Ladle into individual soup bowls and sprinkle with a little paprika and chopped parsley.

Minestrone Soup

STOBO CASTLE

74 kcals per portion • Serves 6

2oz/55g carrots, peeled	2oz/55g tomatoes
2oz/55g celery	1oz/30g spaghetti
2oz/55g onion	1oz/30g fine green beans
2oz/55g leek	1 pint/570ml tomato juice
2oz/55g courgette	1 pint/570ml vegetable stock
2oz/55g aubergine	olive oil
1 clove of garlic	

Cut all vegetables, except the beans into paisan (squares, rounds and triangles about the size of a penny). Sweat vegetables in a little olive oil in a pan. Add crushed and chopped garlic, tomato juice and stock. Simmer for 1 hour adding extra stock in necessary. Add the beans and spaghetti cut or broken into ¹/₂ in/1cm pieces and simmer for 10 minutes. Season to taste and serve immediately.

Mixed Vegetable Soup

SHRUBLAND HALL

70 kcals per portion • Serves 6-8

2 or 3 medium-sized onions, peeled and quartered	2lb/910g cabbage, coarsely chopped
1 leek, washed and roughly chopped, green part included	1oz/30g butter or margarine
	sea salt and black pepper to taste
1¹/₂-2lb/680-910g carrots, scrubbed and coarsely chopped	stock or water to cover

Coarsely chop all the vegetables and put in a large pot with just enough water to cover. Set on moderate heat with lid on pot. Allow to bubble until soft (avoid simmering too gently). Strain and reserve cooking water. Liquidise vegetable pulp with a little butter or margarine. Return to cooking liquid, stir in seasoning and bring gently back to boiling point. Add more water if contents require thinning. Serve immediately.

Mushroom and Tarragon Soup

INGLEWOOD HEALTH HYDRO

38 kcals per portion • Serves 4

1lb /450g mushrooms	1 tablespoon tarragon (fresh or dried)
1/2 pint/285ml chicken stock	1 pint/570ml skimmed milk

Finely chop the mushrooms and put in a saucepan with the stock and half the tarragon. Allow to simmer for 5 minutes, then blend or sieve. Return to the saucepan, add the milk and the remainder of the tarragon. Reheat but do not allow to boil. Serve with a little chopped fresh tarragon or parsley.

Orange and Carrot Soup

HENLOW GRANGE

35 kcals per portion • Serves 4

3oz/85g carrot, chopped	1 bayleaf
1oz/30g onion, chopped	pinch of dried basil
1 stick of celery chopped	finely grated zest of 1 orange
1 pint/570ml vegetable stock	ground black pepper
1/2 pint/285ml fresh orange juice	

Place the vegetables, stock, orange juice, herbs and orange zest in a large pan. Bring to the boil, then cover and simmer until the carrots are tender. Remove and discard the bayleaf. Puree in a food processor, season to taste with freshly ground black pepper. Return to the pan and reheat if necessary. Serve piping hot, garnished with fresh grated carrot or thin strips of orange rind.

Oriental Soup

CEDAR FALLS

70 kcals per portion • Serves 6

32fl oz/1125ml vegetable stock	3oz/85g sliced spring onions
6oz/170g mange tout	4 oz/115g carrot (cut into thin strips)
3oz/85g sliced mushrooms	2 tablespoons rice wine vinegar

Prepare stock. Clean mange tout, remove strings and slice in half crossways. Chop mushrooms and spring onions. Prepare and shape carrots. Bring stock to boil, add carrots, spring onions, mange tout and mushrooms and cook for 2 or 3 minutes. Just prior to serving, stir in rice wine vinegar. (For a more substantial soup, making 171 kcals per portion, add 10oz/285g dried cooked ham).

Parsnip Heart of the Country Soup

HOAR CROSS HALL

100 kcals per portion • Serves 4

2 leeks	1 large potato
1 parsnip (about 6oz/170g)	sea salt and pepper
2 tablespoons vegetable oil	watercress leaves for garnish
1½ pints/900ml vegetable stock	

Wash and trim leeks and parsnips, cut fairly small and saute in oil for 5 to 10 minutes. Add stock, sliced potato and seasoning. Simmer until tender, do not overcook. Puree down and only reheat before serving. Garnish with watercress leaves.

Potato, Onion and Celery Soup

INGLEWOOD HEALTH HYDRO

92 kcals per portion • Serves 4

10oz/285g potatoes	8oz/225g carrots
2 small onions	½ teaspoon dried thyme
1 clove garlic	1 teaspoon chervil or parsley
4 sticks celery	2 pints/1.2 litres water or chicken stock
2 tablespoons tomato puree	salt and pepper

Peel potatoes, onions and garlic. Clean celery and carrots and chop all vegetables roughly and put in large saucepan with the water or stock. Stir in tomato puree and thyme. Bring to boil and simmer on low heat for an hour. Blend or strain and heat through and add salt and pepper to taste. Serve sprinkled with chervil or parsley.

Smoked Haddock Soup

RAGDALE HALL

90 kcals per portion • Serves 4

15fl oz/505ml skimmed milk	8oz/225g smoked haddock
10fl oz/330ml fish stock or water	pinch of nutmeg
2oz/55g chopped onion	

Flake the haddock into a saucepan and remove any bones. Add remaining ingredients, bring to the boil and simmer for 30 minutes. Remove from heat and liquidise soup until smooth and creamy in a blender or food processor. Reheat and season to taste, thicken if necessary with a little cornflour mixed with water.

Spinach and Blue Cheese Soup

STOBO CASTLE

90 kcals per portion • Serves 6

5oz/140g spinach	1/4 crushed clove of garlic
1 1/2 oz/45g blue cheese	8fl oz/285ml skimmed milk
1oz/30g peeled and diced onion	1 pint/570ml water

Place the spinach, onion and garlic in a saucepan and sweat for 5 to10 minutes. Add the milk and water and bring to the boil. Crumble the blue cheese into the soup and simmer for 5 minutes. Remove from the heat and liquidise the soup for 30 seconds. Season to taste and serve.

Summer Gazpacho

CHAMPNEYS

88 kcals per portion • Serves 4

3 1/2 oz/100g onions	2oz/55g fresh breadcrumbs
3 1/2 oz/100g cucumber	1 teaspoon red wine vinegar
3 1/2 oz/100g red and green peppers,	1 clove garlic, freshly diced
1 pint/570ml tomato juice	sea salt and freshly milled black pepper
3fl oz/85ml fresh orange juice	4 tablespoons mixed peppers,
dash of lemon juice	finely diced for garnish

Put all the ingredients (except the diced pepper for the garnish) in a blender or food processor and liquidise until well blended. Chill in the refrigerator and serve cold, garnished with the diced peppers.

Sweetcorn and Coriander Soup

FOREST MERE

70 kcals per portion • Serves 4

1oz/30g unsalted butter	1 red pepper, seeded and chopped
1 tablespoon sunflower oil	1 ripe tomato, seeded and chopped
3 cloves garlic	12oz/340g sweetcorn kernels
1 onion finely chopped	1 pint/570ml vegetable stock
1 teaspoon ground cumin	2 tablespoons coriander, chopped
1 sweet green pepper, seeded and chopped	salt and pepper
1 green chilli pepper, seeded and chopped	

Heat the oil, add garlic, onion and cumin. After 5 minutes add the peppers followed by the tomatoes and sweetcorn. Cook for a further 4 to 5 minutes. Add the stock and check the seasoning. Add the chopped coriander and serve.

Tomato and Basil Soup

HENLOW GRANGE

57 kcals per portion • Serves 4

2lb/910g fresh tomatoes	10-15 basil leaves
1 small onion	2 teaspoons tomato puree
1 small clove of garlic	1½ pints/900ml vegetable stock
2oz/55g carrot	½ teaspoon caster sugar
2oz/55g celery	(or artificial sweetener)

Roughly chop the tomatoes, onion, garlic, carrot and celery. Place in a large saucepan and add the basil, tomato puree, stock, freshly ground pepper and sugar. Bring to the boil, then cover and simmer for 20 minutes, until the vegetables are very soft. Puree in a food processor, then sieve. Adjust seasoning as required and serve hot.

Watercress and Potato Soup

STOBO CASTLE

90 kcals per portion • Serves 6

1lb/450g floury potatoes (eg Golden Wonder) cut into ½ in/1cm dice	2 pints/1.12 litres vegetable stock
3 bunches watercress	sprig of fresh thyme
1 medium size onion	salt and ground pepper

Retain a dozen or so small sprigs from the tops of the watercress for the garnish, and finely chop the remainder with the onion. Fry very quickly in a hot, slightly oiled pan, stirring continuously to ensure that the onion does not take on a colour. Add to the boiling vegetable stock and potatoes and bring back to the boil, adding the fresh thyme. Simmer for 15 minutes. Remove thyme and liquidise. Season to taste and serve garnished with watercress leaves.

Supreme of Chicken with Passion Fruit Sauce, Ragdale Hall

Baby Chicken with Mint and Pineapple
Forest Mere
400 kcals approximately • Serves 4

2 x 1lb/450g poussins	2 tablespoons chopped mint
6oz/170g bulgar wheat	1/2oz/15g butter
2 oranges	salt and pepper
1 small pineapple	4 cloves garlic
4 spring onions	

First make the stuffing: Cover the bulgar wheat in boiling water for 10 minutes and then drain well. Grate the orange rind, segment the oranges, peel the pineapple, chop up half and slice the remainder for garnish. Thinly slice the spring onion and crush the garlic. Melt the butter in a pan and cook onion, garlic, pineapple and orange for 5 or 6 minutes. Add to the strained bulgar wheat with half the chopped mint and season well. Prepare the poussin and fill with the stuffing. Brush each bird with a little oil and roast for in a moderate oven 350°F/180°C/Gas Mark 4 for 45 minutes. Mix grated orange rind with pan juices and baste the birds, cooking for a further 5 minutes. Heat the pineapple slices thoroughly, coat in the remaining chopped mint and use to garnish the birds. Half poussin per portion.

Breast of Chicken - Coq au Leekie
Hoar Cross Hall
350 kcals (large portion) • Serves 1

1 medium breast of chicken	2fl oz/70ml chicken stock
1oz/30g salmon	1fl oz/35ml cream (optional)
2oz/55g cooked leek (diced)	1 egg white
½ raw leek	salt and pepper

Remove fillet from breast and beat out flat. Mince or puree down the salmon, add egg white and seasoning to produce a mousse. Add cooked, diced leek to the mousse. Fill mousse into chicken and cover with flattened chicken fillet. Poach in chicken stock for 5 to10 minutes. Cook the half leek and puree down. Add leek puree to chicken stock, add cream if required, season and reduce to a sauce consistency. Serve piping hot with seasonal vegetables.

Chicken Breast Stuffed with Carrots, Leeks and Black Olives with a Tomato Vinaigrette
Champneys
298 kcals per portion • Serves 4

4 x 5oz/140g chicken breasts	Vinaigrette:
2 carrots, peeled and grated	3 large, ripe tomatoes
1 large leek, finely chopped	2 tablespoons extra virgin olive oil
16 black olives	1 fresh basil leaf
sea salt	1 tablespoon cider vinegar
freshly milled black pepper	Garnish: chervil sprigs and 2 leeks,
1 pint/570ml fresh chicken stock	blanched in strips

Skin chicken breasts and remove fillets. Bang fillets lightly with a knife to flatten. Make small incision into chicken breast to form a pocket. Season grated carrot, chopped leek and chopped olives with salt and pepper and stuff the chicken breast with the mixture. Lay the fillets over the mixture and pull the pockets over to seal the breast and put in an ovenproof dish. Heat chicken stock to boiling and pour over breasts. Cook in hot oven for 10 minutes. Meanwhile, liquidise all the ingredients for the sauce in a food processor and pass through a fine sieve. When the chicken is cooked, sear with a very hot skewer to make a diamond pattern, then slice diagonally and place on plate. Serve the vinaigrette sauce around the sliced chicken breast, garnished with sprigs of chervil and bundles of blanched leeks.

Chicken Pilaff

INGLEWOOD

A quick and tasty way to use cooked chicken left-overs,
far more interesting than a cold chicken salad!
320 kcals per portion • Serves 4

6oz/170g cooked chicken	2 tablespoons oil
6oz/170g long grain rice	1/2 pint/285ml chicken stock
6oz/170g sweetcorn	pinch of ground cardamon
1 medium onion	*or* seeds of one cardamon
1 green pepper	pinch of ground ginger

Heat the oil and add the finely chopped onions. Cook gently for about 5 minutes. Add the rice and, stirring continuously, cook for another 5 minutes. Chop the green pepper and add this and the spices, stir well, then gradually add the chicken stock. Simmer for about 15 minutes until the rice is tender. Add the chicken cut into small pieces and the sweetcorn, heat through and serve.

Chicken Supreme with Orange and Lemon

GRAYSHOTT HALL

A luxurious chicken dish, simple to prepare and cook,
with a refreshingly different tangy sauce.
280 kcals per portion • Serves 4

4 x 6oz/170g chicken breasts	1/2 oz/15g cornflour, mixed with a little water
juice of 4 oranges	2 tablespoons sugar
juice of 2 lemons	1/4 pint/150ml wine vinegar
1/2 pint/285ml chicken stock	4 tablespoons creme fraiche

First make the sauce in a pan by boiling together all the ingredients except the chicken portions and creme fraiche. Grill the chicken breasts until just cooked, carve on the slant and place on warmed plates. Heat the sauce, whisk in the creme fraiche and pour over the chicken. Serve immediately.

Chinese Stir Fry
HENLOW GRANGE

This recipe makes a substantial main course and is very simple to prepare despite its long list of ingredients.
280 kcals per portion • Serves 4

1lb/450g fillet of beef	1 green pepper, de-seeded and sliced
1 tablespoon olive oil	1 x 8oz/225g can waterchestnuts,
1 teaspoon sesame oil	drained and sliced
1 medium onion, sliced	2oz/55g mushrooms, sliced
1 clove garlic, chopped	6 spring onions, trimmed and sliced
2in/5cm piece of fresh ginger,	4oz/115g Chinese leaf, shredded
peeled and shredded	4oz/115g beansprouts
1 red pepper, de-seeded and sliced	2 tablespoons dark soy sauce

Prepare all the ingredients. Flatten beef with a rolling pin and cut into strips. Heat the olive oil and sesame oil in a wok or large deep frying pan until smoking. Add beef and stir fry to seal very quickly. Transfer to warmed plate. Add onion, garlic and ginger and stir fry for a minute, then add the peppers, waterchestnuts, mushrooms and spring onions and stir fry for a further minute. Return the beef to the pan and add the Chinese leaf, beansprouts and soy sauce. Stir fry for a further minute before serving immediately.

Fillet of Beef with an Oatmeal Crust
RAGDALE HALL

The oatmeal topping makes this a healthy as well as luxurious dish.
275 kcals per portion • Serves 4

4 x 5oz/140g lean fillets of beef	2fl oz/70ml skimmed milk
1½oz/45g oatmeal	1 teaspoon freshly chopped parsley
2oz/55g mushrooms	1 teaspoon light sunflower oil
½oz/15g Stilton cheese	*Garnish:* watercress and lightly cooked
1 stick celery	wild mushrooms

Finely dice the mushrooms and celery and sweat for 2 minutes in the sunflower oil. Transfer to a bowl and add the oats and parsley. Crumble the Stilton into the bowl and mix the ingredients together. Slowly add the milk to bind the mixture and then divide into four equal portions. Grill the fillets of beef to your preference, top each one with a portion of oat mixture and grill for a further 5 minutes until crisp. Serve garnished with watercress and some lightly cooked wild mushrooms.

Fillet Steak Medallions with Peppercorns

HENLOW GRANGE

210 kcals per portion • Serves 4

1lb/450g fillet of beef cut into 8 medallions	1 pint/570ml beef stock
1 tablespoon sunflower oil	6 tablespoons red wine
1 small onion, finely diced	2 teaspoons wholegrain mustard
3 teaspoons green or pink peppercorns	fresh herbs to garnish

Pan fry each medallion of beef in hot oil for 30 seconds each side to seal and brown the meat. Transfer to plate. Pour off excessive oil and add onion and peppercorns and cook until onions are soft. Add wine and cook until it has reduced by half. Return meat to pan, pour on stock and cook rapidly to reduce liquid by half again. Sauce should now be glossy. Transfer meat to serving plates. Stir the mustard into sauce and spoon over medallions of beef. Garnish with fresh herbs.

Hot Spiced Pork in Mustard Sauce

SPRINGS HYDRO

A tasty and unusual way to enjoy pork
255 kcals per portion • Serves 4

1lb/450g lean loin of pork	5 tablespoons dry white wine
1 teaspoon cayenne pepper	1 teaspoon cornflour
1 medium onion, sliced	2 tablespoons wholegrain mustard
2oz/55g button mushrooms, sliced	2 teaspoons Worcestershire sauce
1/2 pint/285ml skimmed milk	

Cut the pork into 4 x 4oz/115g slices. Place between 2 sheets of greaseproof paper and beat out with a rolling pin. Season with cayenne pepper. Dry fry the pork in a non-stick pan for 1 minute each side. Transfer to a plate. Add the onions and mushrooms to the pan and cook for 2 minutes. Pour on the milk, and add the wine blended with the cornflour, mustard and Worcestershire sauce. Bring to the boil, stirring, until the mixture thickens slightly. Return the meat to the sauce and simmer for 15 to 20 minutes or until the pork is tender, then serve.

Lamb and Rice with Apricots
INGLEWOOD

An ideal recipe for using up left-over roast lamb.
386 kcals per portion • Serves 4

8oz/225g long grain rice
1 medium onion
1oz/30g butter or margarine
8oz/225g cooked lamb
1 tablespoon raisins
2oz/55g dried apricots

¹/₂ teaspoon crushed coriander seeds
¹/₂ teaspoon crushed cumin seeds
¹/₂ teaspoon ground cinnamon
salt and pepper
1 tablespoon orange flower water
(to serve)

Wash and boil the rice until tender. Finely chop the onion and cut the lamb into small pieces. Finely chop the dried apricots. Melt the butter in a heavy pan. Add the lamb, the onion, fruit and spices and cook gently until the onion is soft. Season with salt and pepper and add the rice mixing the ingredients together. Heat through and serve with the orange flower water and a few more raisins sprinkled on top.

Lasagnette with Chicken, Mango and Raisins
FOREST MERE

280 kcals per portion • Serves 4

8oz/225g cooked chicken, cubed
1 onion, finely chopped
1 tablespoon olive oil
1 crushed clove of garlic
¹/₂ pint/285ml chicken stock
1 mango, peeled and chopped
2 tablespoons chopped parsley

2oz/55g raisins
¹/₄ teaspoon each of ground clove,
cinnamon and cumin
1 teaspoon ground turmeric
¹/₂ teaspoon toasted cardamon seeds
8oz/225g cooked narrow lasagnette
(or other) pasta

Put the chicken in a bowl, sprinkle with the spices and toss well. Allow to stand for 30 minutes. Heat the oil and saute the onion and garlic, add the chicken and fry until golden. Add the stock, mango and raisins and cook slowly for 20 minutes. Season with salt and cayenne pepper to taste. Combine with the cooked pasta, sprinkle with the parsley and serve immediately.

Meatballs in Rich Mushroom Sauce

CEDAR FALLS

278 kcals per portion • Serves 2

	Mushroom sauce:
12oz/340g minced steak	2 bacon rashers finely chopped
1 medium onion, finely chopped	(for extra flavour used smoked)
1 clove garlic, crushed	4oz/115g mushrooms, thinly sliced
1 tablespoon tomato puree	1/2 pint/285ml vegetable stock
1 tablespoon soya sauce	1 teaspoon fresh basil, shredded
4oz/115g breadcrumbs	
2 teaspoons oil	

Combine mince, onions, garlic, tomato puree, soya sauce and breadcrumbs. Shape into 4 large or 8 small balls. Refrigerate for 30 minutes. Cook gently in a frying pan with the oil until nicely browned and cooked in the middle. Transfer to a warmed plate. Make the sauce in the same pan by adding bacon and mushrooms and cooking until mushrooms are tender. Stir in blended cornflour and water with the vegetable stock, boil until sauce thickens. Return meatballs to the pan, add basil and simmer until heated through and serve at once.

Mustard Rabbit

INGLEWOOD

Try this savoury rabbit dish as a change from chicken. Despite being so tasty and low in fat, many people in the UK have never tried rabbit.

300 kcals per portion • Serves 4

2lb/910g rabbit pieces	3 tablespoons Dijon mustard
4 carrots	large bunch of parsley and thyme,
1 medium onion	finely chopped
1 clove garlic	4fl oz/150ml dry white wine
3oz/85g low-fat cheese	1/2 pint/285ml chicken stock

Chop the carrots and onion finely, crush the garlic and place in the bottom of a heavy casserole. Place the rabbit joints on top. Sprinkle on the thyme and a little of the parsley. Add the wine, the stock (use a chicken stock cube) and cover. Cook in a pre-heated medium oven (325°F, 170°C, Gas Mark 3) for around 2 hours until the rabbit is cooked. Remove meat and vegetables to a heated serving dish and return to low oven to keep warm. Take the cooking juice, skim off any fat and reduce in a pan until about 4 tablespoonsl remain. Allow these to cool and blend with the low-fat cheese and mustard. Add nearly all the remaining parsley. Serve the rabbit sprinkled with the rest of the parsley and the sauce served separately.

Noisette of Lamb with Reform Sauce
Ragdale Hall
260 kcals per portion • Serves 4

4 x 4oz/115g lean noisettes of lamb	1 teaspoon malt vinegar
6fl oz/170ml brown beef stock	2 teaspoons cornflour
2 small cooked beetroot	4 sprigs of rosemary
2 hard boiled egg whites	4 cherry tomatoes - cut in half crossways
2oz/55g lamb's tongue	1 tablespoon light sunflower oil
2 gherkins	salt and pepper
1 onion, peeled and diced	

Place the noisettes on a baking tray, brush with a little oil and season. Bake at 350°F, 180°C, Gas Mark 4 for 15 to 20 minutes until cooked pink. Cut the egg whites, beetroot, tongue and gherkins into small thin strips. To make the sauce heat up the oil and sweat the onion for 5 minutes. Add the beef stock, vinegar, egg whites, tongue, beetroot and gherkin and bring to the boil. Mix the corn-flour with a little water and stir into the sauce to thicken. Simmer for 2 to 3 minutes. Serve the noisettes smothered with the reform sauce and garnished with rosemary and cherry tomatoes.

Orange Roast Lamb
Forest Mere
300 kcals approximately • Serves 4

1 leg of lamb boned and rolled	2 or 3 onions chopped
2 tablespoons Worcestershire sauce	juice of $\frac{1}{2}$ lemon
grated rind and juice of 2 oranges	2oz/55g soft brown sugar

Place the Worcestershire sauce, orange and lemon plus the sugar in a saucepan and heat gently stirring until the sugar has dissolved. Place the joint of lamb on a bed of onions. Pour the glaze over the joint and cook for approximately 2 hours at 400°F, 200°C, Gas Mark 5. Baste at regular intervals. To serve use the pan juices plus a little stock or vegetable water to de-glaze the cooking tin, season and strain.

Sirloin Steak with Tarragon and Mustard Sauce
GRAYSHOTT HALL
280 kcals per portion • Serves 4

4 x 6oz/170g sirloin steaks, trimmed of all fat and sinew

1/4 pint/285ml strong brown beef stock

1 teaspoon cornflour, thinned with water

1 tablespoon creme fraiche

2 teaspoons French mustard

1 tablespoon tarragon, chopped

watercress sprigs to garnish

Heat the stock to boiling, thicken with cornflour and reboil. Whisk in the creme fraiche, mustard and tarragon. Grill the steaks to taste, season and serve garnished, with the sauce.

Supreme of Chicken with Passion Fruit Sauce
RAGDALE HALL
210 kcals per portion • Serves 4

4 x 6oz/170g skinned chicken breasts

15fl oz/535ml chicken stock

3 passion fruits

1 glass of dry white wine

4 sprigs of dill to garnish

In a large saucepan, bring the chicken stock to the boil and poach the supremes for approximately 15 to 20 minutes. Remove and keep hot while preparing the sauce. Scoop out the passion fruit flesh and seeds into a medium sized saucepan and add the chicken stock and wine. Simmer until reduced to a coating consistency (should coat the back of a spoon). Serve the supremes on top of the sauce and garnish with a sprig of dill.

Turkey Roulade with Cranberry Sauce
SPRINGS HYDRO
239 kcals per portion • Serves 4

4 x 4oz/115g turkey escalopes

2oz/55g sage and onion stuffing

2oz/55g mushrooms, chopped

1/4 pint/150ml red wine

1/4 pint/150ml chicken or turkey stock

3oz/85g cranberry sauce

1/2 teaspoon dried mixed herbs

ground black pepper

Preheat oven to 375°F, 190°C, Gas Mark 5. Place the escalopes between 2 sheets of greaseproof paper and flatten with a rolling pin. Mix together the sage and onion stuffing and mushrooms. Add enough boiling water to form a firm stuffing. Place the stuffing at one end of each escalope and roll up. Lay, seal down, in a shallow dish and bake for 5 minutes to set the rolls. Remove from the oven. Make the sauce by heating the red wine and stock in a small pan. Add the cranberry sauce, herbs and ground black pepper and stir until the sauce has melted. Pour over the turkey rolls, return to the oven and cook for a further 20 minutes. Serve each roll, sliced, accompanied with the sauce.

Baked Trout with a Hazelnut and Lemon Sauce, Ragdale Hall

Baked Herring with Tomatoes
INGLEWOOD
262 kcals per portion • Serves 4

4 herrings	1lb/450g tomatoes
2 medium onions	2 bay leaves
1oz/30g butter	2 teaspoons fresh dill or parsley
2 teaspoons mild Dijon mustard	low-calorie sweetener
4fl oz/115ml white wine vinegar	salt and pepper

Ask the fishmonger to remove the herring head and backbone and slit down the side. Open fish and sprinkle in some of the dill with the salt and pepper. Cut onions into fine slices and sweat in the butter, add the mustard, vinegar and a little low-calorie sweetener. Put the herrings into a baking dish and pour on the liquid and onions. Add the bay leaves and cook in a medium oven 350°F, 180°C, Gas Mark 4 for 10 minutes. Add the tomatoes, cut into quarters and cook for another 30 minutes until fish are tender.

Baked Trout with a Hazelnut and Lemon Sauce
RAGDALE HALL
195 kcals per portion • Serves 4

4 x 5oz/140g cleaned rainbow trout	1 tablespoon freshly chopped coriander
1oz/30g low fat spread	salt and pepper
juice of 2 lemons	

Place the trout in a deep baking tray and season with freshly milled salt and pepper. Cover with water and cook in an oven pre-heated to 350°F, 180°C, Gas Mark 4 for 10-15 minutes. Make the sauce by gently melting the spread and adding hazelnuts, lemon juice and coriander. Gently simmer for 2 minutes. When the trout are cooked, remove the head, tail and skin. Arrange onto serving plates and drizzle the sauce over the trout. Serve accompanied by minted boiled potatoes.

Creole Cod Fillet

GRAYSHOTT HALL

A deliciously different way of serving cod steaks -
marinate for 2 to 3 hours to allow the subtle spicy flavours to permeate.
88 kcals per portion • Serves 4

4 x 6oz/170g cod steaks	2 tablespoons olive oil
20 peppercorns	juice of 1 lime
10 allspice berries	juice of 3 oranges
1 teaspoon coriander seeds	1 tablespoon chopped coriander
2 dried chillies	*Garnish:* lime wedges and coriander sprigs
2 cloves of garlic	

Crush the peppercorns, allspice, coriander seeds, chillies and garlic to a paste. Rub the fish with the mixture and marinate for 2 to 3 hours. Brush the steaks with oil and grill for 3 to 4 minutes each side or until cooked. Heat the orange and lime juice, add the chopped coriander and pour over the fish. Serve immediately.

Fillet of Pink Trout with Watercress Puree

STOBO CASTLE

The pink flesh of the trout and the green tones of the watercress puree
make a pleasing contrast in this easily prepared dish.
70 kcals per portion • Serves 4

4 x 8oz/225g rainbow trout	3 bunches of watercress
(cleaned with head and tail removed)	1 small onion
1 lemon	4fl oz/150ml vegetable or fish stock
2 or 3 fresh sorrel leaves (when available)	salt and pepper

Remove 8 full leaves of watercress for garnish, and blanch for several seconds in boiling water then freshen under cold water. Pouch the trout in approximately 2 pints/1.12 litres of well salted water with the juice of the lemon added for about 8 minutes. To make the coulis, chop the onion and watercress and saute in a very hot pan lightly wiped with olive oil. Stir continuously until the watercress adopts a richer green colour (about 3 minutes). Add the stock and bring to the boil. Liquidise immediately with sorrel leaves (if used) and adjust seasoning to taste. Remove the skin from the trout and place on the coulis. Garnish the pink flesh with the blanched watercress.

Haddock Fillets with Coriander and Orange

GRAYSHOTT HALL

220 kcals per portion • Serves 4

4 x 6oz/170g haddock fillets, skinned

1 tablespoon sesame seeds

2 tablespoons ground coriander seeds

finely grated rind and juice of 2 large oranges

1 tablespoon olive oil

¹/₂ pint/285ml fish stock

1 teaspoon cornflour, thinned with a little water

4 tablespoons creme fraiche

salt and pepper

Season the haddock fillets. Mix together the sesame seeds, coriander and orange zest. Press the fish into this mixture, brush with oil and grill for 4 to 5 minutes, or until the fish is cooked. Transfer to a warm plate. Boil the stock, thicken with cornflour and stir in creme fraiche. Pour sauce over fish before serving.

Malaysian Fish Curry

INGLEWOOD

A tasty recipe which makes a change from chicken or meat curries and requires a shorter cooking time. Although the recipe is for cod, any other white fish may be used.

233 kcals per portion • Serves 4

4 x 6oz/170g cod steaks

2 medium onions

1 teaspoon coriander seeds

1 teaspoon cumin seeds

¹/₂ teaspoon chilli powder

1 teaspoon tumeric

1 teaspoon grated ginger root

1 teaspoon curry powder

1 tablespoon vegetable oil

¹/₄ pint/150ml skimmed milk

4 pineapple rings, fresh or tinned

Crush all the dried spices together in a pestle and mortar (or electric grinder). Finely chop the onions and sweat in the oil. Add the spices and mix well together. Add the milk gradually, stirring well. Add the fish (frozen fish should be defrosted in a little of the milk and then drained) and cook gently for about 10 minutes, stirring regularly. Serve with rings of fresh or tinned pineapple and boiled rice, allowing 1oz/30g rice per person (100 kcals) and 30 calories per slice of pineapple.

Medallions of Monkfish au Poivre

HOAR CROSS HALL

Monkfish is popular in Europe, but still relatively unknown in the UK.
Its firm white flesh makes excellent kebabs for the barbecue, can be served cold with salads, or
cooked as fish steaks - as in this imaginative recipe.
150 kcals per portion • Serves 2

2 x 3oz/85g monkfish medallions	1 tablespoon red wine
2oz/55g spring cabbage	6 green peppercorns, crushed
4fl oz/150ml beef stock	pepper and salt
1fl oz/35ml fish stock	1fl oz/35ml olive oil

Pan fry the monkfish medallions in small amount of olive oil and seasoning. Remove when coated and keep warm. Add red wine and crushed peppercorns to pan followed by fish and beef stock and reduce by half. In a separate pan saute off the spring cabbage. Put the cabbage on a plate with the medallions on top and glace with sauce. Serve immediately.

Red Mullet with Salad Nicoise

CHAMPNEYS

This exotic fish has a wonderful scarlet colour and flavour.
Not to be confused with grey mullet, which is cheaper and good in its own right,
but does not have such a fine flavour.
323 kcals per portion • Serves 4

4 x 8oz/225g fillets of red mullet, scaled	1 tablespoon extra virgin olive oil
juice of $^1/_2$ lime	2 small potatoes
2 shallots, finely chopped	sea salt and freshly milled black pepper
2$^1/_2$ oz/70g mange tout, blanched and sliced	*Sauce:* 2 tablespoons cider vinegar
10 black olives, stoned and chopped	pinch of saffron powder
4 large tomatoes, skinned, de-seeded and finely chopped	1 tablespoon extra virgin olive oil

Prepare the salad by mixing the shallots, mangetout, olives and two-thirds of the diced tomato in a large bowl with the olive oil and lightly season. Peel the potatoes and cut into 6 x $^1/_4$ in/6mm dice. Boil until cooked, about 15 minutes. Allow to cool and add the potatoes to the vegetable mixture. To make the sauce, reduce the cider vinegar and saffron over a high heat by two-thirds and stir in the olive oil. Season the red mullet fillets with the lime juice and some black pepper and grill, skin-side up, for 4 minutes. To serve, place a quarter of the salad nicoise in the centre of each plate, top with a red mullet fillet and pour a little sauce over the fish. Garnish with the remaining diced tomato.

Salmon and Herb Loaf

FOREST MERE

This nutritious recipe makes a great 'high tea' or supper dish.
It tastes especially good accompanied by a green salad,
some freshly baked crusty bread and a pot of tea.
400 kcals per portion • Serves 4

1lb/450g cooked salmon	1 teaspoon Worcestershire sauce
2oz/55g stale bread crumbs	2 tablespoons lemon juice
3 sticks celery, finely chopped	1 teaspoon dry mustard
6 spring onions, finely chopped	1/4 pint/150ml milk
3 x size 2 eggs, separated	1/2oz/15g butter

Combine all the ingredients in a bowl (except the eggs, milk and butter), mix well and season. Warm the milk and butter together until the butter has melted, cool, add to fish mixture with egg yolks and mix well. Beat egg whites to form soft peaks and fold into the fish mixture. Transfer to greased loaf tin and bake for 50 minutes at 400°F, 200°C, Gas Mark 5 or until firm to touch. Cool for about 10 minutes before turning out. Serve warm with a herb dressing and salad. Make a herb dressing by combining fresh chopped mixed herbs (parsley, dill, mint, chives) with mixture of half mayonnaise and half French dressing.

Sole Fillets with Pepper Sauce

HENLOW GRANGE

The red pepper sauce transforms this dish into something special.
165 kcals per portion • Serves 4

1lb/450g sole fillets, skinned	3/4 pint/425ml fish stock
1lb/450g red peppers	1/4 pint/150ml dry white wine
1 small onion, diced	ground black pepper
1 clove garlic, crushed	*Garnish:* 1 lemon
1 bayleaf	

Dice the red pepper, discarding the seeds. Dry fry in a pan with the onion, garlic and bayleaf. Pour on the stock and white wine, bring to the boil then simmer for 20 to 30 minutes or until the peppers are very soft. Remove the bayleaf, then liquidise or puree the peppers until smooth. Return to the rinsed out pan, season to taste with freshly ground black pepper and reheat. Place the fillets on a non-stick frying pan or baking tray and squeeze the lemon juice over them. Cook under a preheated grill for 4 to 5 minutes. To serve, coat each plate with red pepper sauce and place the sole fillets in the centre.

Sole Fillets with Prawns, Grapes and Asparagus

FOREST MERE

220 kcals per portion • Serves 2

6 lemon sole fillets, skinned	2oz/55g spring onions, finely chopped
4oz/115g prawns	2 ripe tomatoes
4oz/115g black grapes	salt and pepper
6oz/170g asparagus tips	juice of 1/2 lemon

De-seed the grapes, blanch the asparagus, skin, de-seed and chop the tomatoes. Fill each sole fillet with prawns, grapes, asparagus, onions and tomatoes. Sprinkle with a little seasoning. Roll up each fillet and secure with cocktail sticks. Place in a baking dish and drizzle with lemon juice. Cover dish with a lid or foil and bake for 15 minutes at 400°F, 200°C, Gas Mark 5. The juices may be strained and served over the fish or thickened slightly and finished either with a spot of whipping cream or a tiny amount of tomato puree. Remove cocktails sticks before serving.

Steamed Mackerel with Tomato and Black Olive Sauce

SPRINGS HYDRO

*Mackerel is a cheap and highly nutritious fish
containing valuable amounts of health giving Omega-3 fatty acids
and vitamins A and D.*
320 kcals per portion • Serves 4

4 x 4oz/115g fresh mackerel fillets	1/2 pint/285ml fish stock
1 small onion, diced	1 clove garlic, chopped
1 small carrot, diced	1 bayleaf, crumbled
1 tablespoon plain flour	ground black pepper
1 x 14oz/400g can tomatoes	2oz/55g black olives, pitted and stoned
2 teaspoons tomato puree	*Garnish:* fresh basil

In a non-stick pan, dry fry the onions and carrots for a few minutes. Sprinkle on the flour and stir for a further minute. Add the tomatoes, puree, stock, garlic and bayleaf. Bring to the boil, then reduce the heat and simmer for 35-45 minutes. Liquidise or puree the sauce, then sieve into a small pan and keep warm until required. Cut each mackerel fillet in half lengthways. Lay one length at a slight angle or twist over its other half. Steam for approximately 7 to 10 minutes or until cooked. Carefully transfer to serving plate. Slice the black olives into the tomato sauce. Season to taste with freshly ground black pepper. Spoon over the fish. Garnish with fresh basil.

Steamed Smoked Salmon with Spinach and Nutmeg Sauce

SPRINGS HYDRO

315 kcals per portion • Serves 4

1lb/450g salmon fillet	1/2 pint/285ml skimmed milk
4oz/115g smoked salmon slices	1/4 pint/150ml fish stock
1 medium onion, diced	pinch of freshly grated nutmeg
4oz/115g young spinach leaves, chopped	ground black pepper
1 teaspoon cornflour	*Garnish:* lemon and fresh herbs

Cut the salmon fillet into 4 neat portions. Wrap the smoked salmon slices around each portion to form a parcel. Steam over water or poach in the fish stock for 10 minutes until firm and cooked. Meanwhile, fry dry the onion in a non-stick frying pan. Add the washed spinach leaves and cook for a further minute or two, until the spinach wilts. Blend a tablespoon of milk with the cornflour. Pour the remainder onto the spinach together with the fish stock. Stir in the blended cornflour and nutmeg. Bring to the boil, stirring, until slightly thickened. Puree the spinach sauce until smooth. Return to the pan and heat through. Season to taste with freshly ground black pepper. Serve the salmon on individual plates with the sauce poured around it. Garnish with fresh herbs and lemon slices.

Tagliolini with Prawns and Radicchio

FOREST MERE

450 kcals per potion • Serves 4

1lb/450g tagliolini pasta cooked	8oz/225g lettuce
2 1/2oz/70g butter	1 small glass brandy
1lb/450g cooked prawns	1/4 pint/150ml single or non-dairy cream
8oz/225g radicchio	salt and black pepper

Heat the butter, add the prawns and shredded lettuce and radicchio leaves. Cook for 5 minutes, add the brandy followed by the cream and seasoning. Add the cooked pasta, stir well and serve at once.

Vegetable Dishes

Vegetable Korma/ Vegetarian Pizza/Vegetable and Aubergine Galette, Henlow Grange

Apricot and Almond Salad
SHRUBLAND HALL

The green and orange colours in this salad are an attractive contrast - as are the ingredients,
the apricots are high calorie and soft in texture, the leaf and cress are low calorie and crisp.
Approximately 360 kcals • Serves 1

fresh or soaked dried apricots	Chinese leaf
(3 or 4 per person)	lemon zest
1oz/30g finely ground almonds	watercress or salad cress
egg yolk	parsley for garnish

Mix together the finely ground almonds with a little lemon zest and enough egg yolk to bind. Halve the apricots and fill with this mixture (about a teaspoonful per half apricot), finishing with a toasted almond flake. Cut a thick slice of Chinese leaf cross-wise, (so that it looks like a piece of Swiss roll). Arrange stuffed apricots in a circle around the edge. Finish with a sprig of watercress or parsley, or tuft of salad cress in the centre, then surround with more cress.

Artichoke with Broad Beans
INGLEWOOD
96 kcals per portion • Serves 2

2 globe artichokes	1 tablespoon fresh herbs
8oz/225g shelled broad beans	(dill, parsley or mint)
4oz/115g spring onions, finely chopped	juice of 1 lemon
including stems	

Wash the artichokes, removing the tough, outer leaves and stem. Sprinkle the artichokes with a little lemon juice and lower into boiling salted water containing lemon juice (to prevent the artichokes discolouring). Cover the pan and simmer. Add the broad beans, onions and dill after 15 minutes and continue to cook for another 30 minutes. Serve garnished with more fresh dill.

Avocado Salad

SHRUBLAND HALL

200 kcals per portion • Serves 4

I avocado, stoned and halved	2 teaspoons chopped nuts
2 small red apples	2 large or 4 small celery stalks (keep leaves)
2 teaspoons raisins or sultanas, soaked overnight	2 tablespoons oil and lemon dressing, flavoured with celery salt

Core the apple and cut into small dice, complete with skin. Mix with chopped celery, nuts and raisins. Add lemon dressing and toss lightly. Halve, stone and peel the avocado and rub with lemon. Cut into chunks and add to the salad. Mix gently with the other ingredients to avoid bruising the avocado. Decorate with celery leaves.

Baked Green Omelette

INGLEWOOD

187 kcals per portion • Serves 4

2 leeks	2-3 tablespoons parsley
4oz/115g spinach	fresh herbs - chives, dill, basil, tarragon
6 spring onions	salt and pepper
8 eggs	

Wash the vegetables and herbs carefully, dry and chop. Beat the eggs and add the other ingredients with a pinch of salt and pepper. Pour into a greased flat baking dish and bake in a low oven 325°F, 170°C, Gas Mark 3 for 45 minutes. Raise temperature for the last 5 minutes 375°F, 190°C, Gas Mark 5 to make the top crusty. Serve immeadiately.

Broccoli and Tomato Pasta

FOREST MERE

270 kcals per portion • Serves 4

1lb/450g cooked broccoli	2oz/55g chopped onion
I tablespoon olive oil	large pinch of grated nutmeg
4oz/115g tomato, skinned, de-seeded and chopped	6fl oz/200ml single or non-dairy cream
	8oz/225g cooked pasta bows

Cook the broccoli in boiling salted water until just tender. Remove from the water and refresh. Use the same water to cook the pasta. Heat the olive oil in a pan, add the onions and sweat until soft, do not brown. Add the strained, cooked pasta, broccoli, tomatoes, cream and seasonings. Toss well and serve immediately.

Cauliflower and Pasta Bake

SPRINGS HYDRO

245 kcals per portion • Serves 4

8oz/225g pasta shells, dried	I small leek, shredded finely
8oz/225g cauliflower florets	I teaspoon dried mixed herbs
(or I small cauliflower)	5 tablespoons dry white wine
I small onion, diced	I x 7oz/200g can chopped tomatoes
I clove garlic, crushed	2oz/55g Cheddar cheese, grated

Preheat oven to 400°F, 200°C, Gas Mark 5. Cook the pasta according to manufacturers instructions. Drain. Cook the cauliflower until just tender. Drain. In a medium saucepan, gently dry fry the onion, garlic, leek and mixed herbs for 2 minutes. Add the wine and cook for a further 2 minutes. Pour in the tomatoes and simmer for a further 15 to 20 minutes until the sauce has reduced and thickened slightly. Gently fold in the cooked pasta and cauliflower. Spoon the mixture into a 3 pint/1.75litre ovenproof dish. Sprinkle over the cheese and cook for 15 minutes or until golden brown.

Celeriac and Wild Mushroom Terrine

CHAMPNEYS

92kcals per portion • Serves 14

3½lb/1.5kg courgettes, grated	Ilb/450g mixed wild mushrooms
3lb/1.35kg celeriac, grated	dash of Worcestershire sauce
2 teaspoons extra virgin olive oil	Garnish: 5fl oz/175ml apple puree
2¼lb/1kg onions, roughly chopped	I red pepper, finely chopped
I clove garlic, finely diced	

Line a I litre/2 pint terrine with cling film or plastic wrap. Sweat the grated courgette and celeriac in a large pan with a little salt and pepper until soft. Heat half the olive oil in a separate pan, add the onions, garlic, wild mushrooms (reserve 8 for garnishing) and a dash of Worcestershire sauce. Sweat until the onions become translucent. To assemble the terrine, line the base with a thin layer of courgette and celeriac, then a layer of the mushroom mixture, followed by another layer of courgette and celeriac and so on, until all the ingredients are used up. Wrap cling film or plastic wrap over the top of the terrine, then pierce a few small holes through the film to allow liquid to escape while the terrine is being pressed. Place a heavy weight or dish filled with cold water on top of the terrine and leave in the fridge for 2 hours. Remove terrine from the mould and invert onto a serving plate. Place a generous slice in the centre of each plate, accompanied by the apple puree, the remaining olive oil, reserved mushrooms and chopped red pepper.

Leek and Gruyere Pasta
FOREST MERE
350 kcals per portion • Serves 4

1lb/450g pasta, cooked	large onion, chopped
1lb/450g leeks, washed and chopped	2fl oz/70ml single or non-dairy cream (optional)
2 tablespoons olive oil	few sprigs of parsley, chopped
8oz/225g Gruyere cheese, grated	seasoning

Sweat the onions and the leeks in the olive oil until soft but not coloured. Add half the grated cheese plus the strained cooked pasta. Toss together, season to taste and add the remaining cheese. If desired finish with a little single dairy or vegetable cream and chopped parsley. Serve at once.

Light Nut Roast
SPRINGS HYDRO
300 kcals per portion • Serves 6

4oz/115g hazelnuts	1/4 red or green pepper, diced
4oz/115g almonds	small clove of garlic, chopped
8oz/225g tomatoes, skinned, de-seeded and diced	1 teaspoon mild curry powder
1 medium onion, diced	2 eggs, beaten

Preheat the oven to 350°F, 180°C, Gas Mark 4. Finely chop the nuts. Place in a bowl and add the tomatoes, onion, red or green pepper, garlic and curry powder. Stir in the beaten eggs and mix thoroughly together. Spoon into a 2lb/1kg loaf tin or an 8in/20cm square cake tin and bake for 20 to 30 minutes until firm. Serve warm or chilled.

Mozzarella, Watercress and Orange Salad
INGLEWOOD
242 kcals per portion • Serves 4

6oz/170g Mozzarella cheese	*Dressing:* juice of 2 oranges,
2 bunches of watercress	or 7fl oz/235ml orange juice
2 large oranges	4 teaspoons coarse-grained, mild mustard
	1 teaspoon cumin/caraway seeds (optional)

Cut the cheese into slivers. Peel and pith the orange and cut into chunks and mix with the chopped watercress. Make the sauce by mixing the orange juice with the mustard and add the spices if wanted. Lay the cheese on top and serve with the orange and mustard dressing.

Mushroom Souffle

INGLEWOOD

234 kcals per portion • Serves 2

1oz/30g low-fat spread	8oz/225g mushrooms
1oz/30g wholemeal flour	2 teaspoons fresh tarragon
3 eggs	or 1 teaspoon dried tarragon

Remove the stalks and peel the mushrooms. Wash these peelings and put in a pan with enough water to cover, boil and simmer for 15 minutes. Strain into a measuring jug and add enough water to make ¼ pint/150ml liquid. Discard the boiled peelings. Wash and finely chop the mushrooms and put to one side. Melt the low fat spread in 1 tablespoon water and add the flour to make a roux. Sprinkle in the tarragon and slowly add the stock, stirring well to form a smooth sauce. Add the mushrooms to the sauce and stir well. Separate the eggs and add the yolks to the sauce. Beat the whites until peaks form, fold into the mixture and pour onto a souffle dish. Bake in a pre-heated oven 350°F, 180°C, Gas Mark 4 for 25 minutes.

Pasta with Broad Beans
and Grainy Mustard

FOREST MERE

154 kcals per portion • Serves 4

8 oz/225g spaghetti, cooked	⅓ pint/200ml vegetable stock
8oz/225g plum tomatoes	2 tablespoons grainy mustard
6oz/170g broad beans	1 oz/30g butter
2 spring onions	salt to taste

Cut the tomatoes into thin strips discarding seeds and stalk. Put the stock in a saucepan, add the broad beans and salt and cook for 6 minutes. Thinly slice the spring onions and add to bean mixture after beans have cooked for 6 minutes. Add the mustard, butter and tomatoes and cook for a further minute. Combine the pasta and sauce, toss well and serve immediately.

Root Vegetable Ragoût

RAGDALE HALL

210 kcals per portion • Serves 4

4oz/115g carrots, peeled	5fl oz/175ml vegetable stock
4oz/115g swede, peeled	1 tablespoon olive oil
4oz/115g mooli (white radish), peeled	1 tablespoon fresh oregano, chopped
4oz/115g fennel, peeled	2 teaspoons cornflour
1 onion, sliced	1/2 teaspoon yeast extract
2 tablespoons tomato puree	5oz/140g uncooked wholewheat rice
1 clove garlic, crushed	

Wash the rice thoroughly and cook in boiling water for 25 minutes or until tender. Roughly chop the carrots, swede, mooli and fennel, and sweat in the olive oil with the onion and garlic until soft. Add the vegetable stock, tomato puree, yeast extract and oregano and simmer for 10 to 15 minutes. Mix the cornflour with a little water and stir into the ragout to thicken. Simmer or a further 5 to 10 minutes. Drain the rice and serve with the ragout.

Slimmer's Pineapple Special

SHRUBLAND HALL

approximately 200 kcals • Serves 1

1 small pineapple	a few pine nuts
1 x 4oz/115g carton cottage cheese	high fibre crispbreads

Allow one small pineapple per person. Scoop out the flesh and cut into cubes. Combine cubed pineapple with cottage cheese and a few pine nuts and serve with crisp, high fibre biscuits (no butter or margarine for serious dieters).

Spinach and Cottage Cheese Pasta

FOREST MERE

250 kcals approximately per portion • Serves 4

1lb/450g spaghetti	2 cloves garlic, crushed
1lb/450g washed spinach	1 onion, chopped
8oz/225g cottage cheese	*Garnish:* nutmeg and Parmesan cheese

Saute the chopped onion and crushed garlic for a few minutes. Blanch the spinach for 5 minutes. Cook the spaghetti in boiling water for about 12 minutes. Strain and add to the onion mixture plus the chopped spinach. Add the cottage cheese and season to taste. Garnish with grated nutmeg and a sprinkling of Parmesan cheese.

Stir Fry Vegetables with Noodles

STOBO CASTLE

130 kcals per portion • Serves 4

1 red pepper	3oz/85g carrots
4oz/115g fresh broccoli	4oz/115g egg noodles
2oz/55g mange tout	(poached and refreshed)
1 small onion	soy sauce
1 bunch spring onions	4fl oz/150ml vegetable stock
1 clove garlic	1 teaspoon cornflour

Cut all the vegetables into strips. Stir fry in a lightly oiled wok for 4 to 5 minutes (moving constantly as there is no oil to baste the vegetables). Add the garlic and stir for 1 minute. Add the vegetable stock and soya sauce (to taste). Mix the cornflour with a little water or cold stock and stir into the vegetables. Add the noodles and mix through thoroughly before serving.

Vegetable and Aubergine Galette

HENLOW GRANGE

An assortment of five vegetables plus garlic and herbs
make up this unusual recipe, the main part of which may be prepared
up to two days in advance.
176 kcals per portion • Serves 2

1 medium carrot, chopped	1 tablespoon tomato puree
1 medium onion, chopped	1 pint/570ml vegetable stock
2 sticks celery, chopped	1 medium aubergine
1 clove garlic, chopped	8oz/225g cottage cheese
5 tomatoes, deseeded and diced	1 tablespoon Parmesan cheese, grated
1 bayleaf	5 basil leaves, shredded

Preheat the oven to 350°F, 180°C, Gas Mark 4. Gently fry the carrot, onion, celery and garlic for 5 minutes. Add the chopped tomatoes, bayleaf and tomato puree and cook for a further 5 minutes. Pour on the stock, bring to the boil then simmer for 50 to 60 minutes. Liquidise the sauce, then pass through a sieve and put to one side. (*This part of the recipe may be prepared in advance*). Cut the aubergine into $1/2$ inch/1cm thick slices. Blanch in boiling water for 1 minute, then refresh in cold water and drain. Layer the tomato sauce, aubergine slices, cottage cheese and basil in a 2 pint/1 litre gratin dish, finishing with a layer of tomato sauce. Sprinkle on the Parmesan cheese and bake for 45 minutes until golden.

Vegetable Korma
HENLOW GRANGE

*This makes a substantial vegetarian main dish
or can also be served as a vegetable course with a fish or meat curry.*
96 kcals per portion • Serves 4

I small onion, diced

1oz/30g low fat spread

2 teaspoons mild curry powder

1oz/30g wholemeal flour

1pint/570ml vegetable stock

4oz/150g celery, thickly sliced

4oz/150g carrot, thickly sliced

1/2 small cauliflower

I dessert apple, peeled and cut into chunks

4oz/150g baby corn

4oz/150g mange tout

4oz/150g button mushrooms, halved

fresh herbs, to garnish

Cook the onions in the low fat spread until softened. Sprinkle on the curry powder and flour and cook for a further minute. Gradually blend in the vegetable stock. Bring to the boil, stirring continuously until thickened and smooth. Reduce heat and add the celery, carrot and cauliflower florets and simmer for 10 to 15 minutes. Add the apple, baby corn and mange tout and simmer for a further 5 minutes or until the vegetables are tender. Serve with rice or jacket potatoes, garnished with fresh herbs.

Vegetable Pizza
HENLOW GRANGE

A simple recipe for home-baked pizza.
325 kcals per portion • Serves 4

8oz/225g plain wholemeal flour

1/2 teaspoon baking powder

2oz/55g low fat spread

2oz/55g canned chopped tomatoes, drained

I small clove garlic, chopped

1/4 small onion, diced

2oz/55g button mushrooms, sliced

1/2 teaspoon mixed dried herbs

2oz/55g mature Cheddar cheese, grated

ground black pepper

Make the pizza base using a fork to work together the flour, baking powder and low fat spread. Add enough water to form a soft dough. Cover and allow to rest for 1 hour in the fridge. Preheat the oven to 400°F, 200°C, Gas Mark 6. Roll out to form an 8 inch/20cm circle and transfer onto a non-stick baking tray. Cook for 10 minutes. When baked and cooled, spread the tomatoes and remaining ingredients over the base, finishing with the cheese. Return to the oven and cook for a further 10 to 15 minutes or until golden brown. Serve hot or cold with a fresh green salad.

Vegetarian Haggis with Neeps and Tatties
STOBO CASTLE

*An unusual and tasty alternative haggis - the pearl barley must be soaked for 2 hours
and cooked in fresh water for 20 minutes before using.*
170 kcals per portion • Serves 4

1 medium onion, finely chopped	1/4 level teaspoon ground white pepper
4oz/115g open cup mushrooms, finely chopped	1 pint/570ml vegetable stock
2oz/55g hazel nuts, finely chopped	chopped fresh thyme
2oz/55g oatmeal	2oz/55g pearl barley

Pre-soak the barley for two hours, pour off the water and cook in fresh water for 20 minutes. Saute the onion in a lightly oiled pan until golden brown. Add mushrooms and hazel nuts and cook for 5 minutes. Add the rest of the ingredients and simmer for 5 minutes. Place in an oven proof dish, cover with aluminium foil and bake in the oven for 30 minutes. Serve with mashed neeps (swede) and tatties (potatoes).

Wholemeal Pancake with a Fruit Filling, Ragdale Hall

Apple and Almond Mousse

160 kcals per portion • Serves 4

8oz/225g cooking apples	4 egg whites
1/2oz/15g gelatine	2oz/55g sugar
2oz/55g ground almonds	raspberries and mint leaves to garnish

Peel and core the apples. Stew in a little water until soft (about 15 to 20 minutes) then leave to cool. Melt gelatine in a little water and when dissolved add to the apples. Mix in the ground almonds. Whisk the egg whites with the sugar to form a light meringue. Gently mix the fruit mixture with the meringue and spoon in to four glasses. Leave to set in the fridge for 3 to 4 hours. Garnish with raspberries and mint leaves before serving.

Apple Souffle

INGLEWOOD

192 kcals per portion • Serves 4

3 medium-sized eating apples	5 egg whites
liquid sweetener	1/2 teaspoon cinnamon
2 tablespoons cornflour	grated rind of 1 lemon
3 egg yolks	

Peel and halve the apples, removing the cores. Half cover with water and cook gently in a pan for about 3 to 5 minutes. Remove the apples and put to one side. Boil the apple liquid until there is about 1/3 pt/190ml and sweeten with a little liquid sweetener if the apples are rather tart. Mix the cornflour with an equal amount of cold water until it forms a smooth paste. Gradually add this to the apple water and heat, stirring all the while until it thickens. Remove from the heat. Whip the egg yolks with the lemon and cinnamon and add these to the sauce. Beat the egg whites until they peak and add a little sweetener. Fold the egg whites into the apple mixture. Place in a hot oven 375°F, 190°C, Gas Mark 5 for 30 minutes and serve immediately.

Apricot Roulade with Raspberries

GRAYSHOTT HALL

A splendid dessert to end a dinner party.
Delicious on its own or served with
fromage frais, yoghurt or Mascarpone cream.
150 kcals per portion • Serves 8

For the roulade:	For the filling:
8oz/225g apricots, pureed	1/2 pint/285ml yoghurt
2 eggs	4 teaspoons almonds, flaked and chopped
4 tablespoons cornflour	For the sauce:
3 tablespoons ground almonds	12oz/340g raspberries
Garnish: 24 raspberries, 8 sprigs of mint	1 pint/570ml orange juice

Beat eggs until they have quadrupled in volume. Gently fold in the pureed apricots, ground almonds and cornflour. Spread roulade mixture onto a baking sheet lined with bakewell parchment. Bake in a moderate oven 300°F, 150°C, Gas Mark 2 for approximately 10 minutes or until the centre of the mixture is firm to the touch. Turn out onto a clean cloth and gently peel away the parchment. When cool, spread the yoghurt and chopped flaked almonds to cover the roulade and roll up, starting at the longest edge. Refrigerate for at least 1 hour. To make the sauce, puree the raspberries with the orange juice in a blender, then sieve. To serve, spread the sauce on a plate, cut the roulade into thick slices, serving one per portion. Garnish with fresh raspberries and sprigs of mint.

Baked Apples with Cinnamon Fromage Frais

SPRINGS HYDRO

138 kcals per portion • Serves 4

4 large eating apples	1 teaspoon runny honey
1oz/30g nibbed almonds	4oz/115g natural fromage frais
1oz/30g sultanas	1 teaspoon ground cinnamon (to taste)

Preheat oven to 350°F, 180°C, Gas Mark 4. Remove the cores from the apples and make a shallow slit around the middle of each one. Mix together the almonds, sultanas and honey and divide between the apple cavities. Place in a shallow ovenproof dish, adding just enough water to cover the base of the dish. Cover loosely with foil and bake for approximately 35 to 45 minutes or until soft. Mix together the fromage frais and ground cinnamon. Chill until required. Serve the baking apples warm, accompanied with the fromage frais.

Baked Egg Custard with Fresh Rhubarb

230 kcals • Serves 4

1 pint/570ml milk	1lb/450g rhubarb
3 eggs	water
2oz/55g sugar	sugar (to sweeten rhubarb)
vanilla pod or a few drops of vanilla essence	nutmeg, grated (optional)

Heat milk with vanilla pod and sugar - stir until sugar is dissolved then discard vanilla pod. Beat the eggs well and add the warmed milk. Pour into a greased pie dish and place in a tin half filled with cold water. Bake in a very moderate 300° F, 150° C, Gas Mark 2, oven until set and very lightly browned. If liked, a little nutmeg may be grated on top of custard before putting into the oven. Prepare the rhubarb by removing the leaves and stump - wash and dry and cut into 1in/3cms length pieces. Put a little sugar and water into a sauce pan and allow sugar to dissolve - bring to the boil and boil for 2-3 minutes. Put prepared rhubarb into the syrup and cook gently until soft. Serve with the custard while hot or cold.

Baked Pineapple with Meringue

260 kcals • Serves 4

2 medium pineapples	3 egg whites
lemon juice	6oz/170g caster sugar
1oz/30g sugar	

Bring water and lemon juice to the boil with a little sugar. Peel and core pineapples and cut into cubes. Place pineapple into syrup and cook quickly. Put pineapple into ramekin dishes. Beat the egg white stiffly and fold in the castor sugar. Put meringue mixture in a piping bag or carefully spoon the mixture over the pineapple, making sure the pineapple is completely covered. Sprinkle with castor sugar and place in a cool oven 275° F, 140° C, Gas Mark 1, until the meringue is crisp and a pale biscuit colour (about 30 mins).

Banana en Papillote

CHAMPNEYS

92 kcals per portion • Serves 4

4 small under-ripe bananas   1 vanilla pod, cut into 4

1 cinnamon stick, cut into 4   2 tablespoons carob, grated

4 star anise   3fl oz/105ml pineapple juice

Preheat the oven to 450°F, 230°C, Gas Mark 8. Lightly grease a piece of aluminium foil large enough to cover one banana and place a banana on top. Arrange a piece of cinnamon stick, 1 star anise and a piece of vanilla pod around the banana and sprinkle with grated carob and a quarter of the pineapple juice. Fold up the foil and seal to make an airtight pocket. Repeat the process with the other 3 bananas. Place the sealed bananas on a baking tray and cook in the oven for 3 to 4 minutes alternatively cook on the side of a bonfire. Serve at once.

Creme Reverse

STOBO CASTLE

225 kcals • serves 4

raspberry puree   2oz/55g sugar

(enough to cover base of 4 ramekin dishes)   vanilla pod

1 pint/570ml milk   or a few drops of vanilla essence

3 eggs

Put raspberry puree in 4 ramekin dishes. Heat milk with vanilla pod and sugar - stir until sugar is dissolved then discard vanilla pod. Beat the eggs well, add the warmed milk and pour carefully into the ramekin dishes. Place ramekins in a deep tin with cold water coming half way up the dishes. Cook in a very moderate oven 300° F, 150° C, Gas Mark 2, until set. When cold turn out onto a plate and serve.

Fresh Fruit Brulee

HENLOW GRANGE

128 kcals per portion • Serves 4

8oz/225g mixed fruit   a few drops of vanilla essence

(raspberries, grapes, banana, kiwi, peaches)   8 teaspoons castor sugar

12oz/340g natural fromage frais

Prepare the fruits and divide between 4 individual ramekin dishes. Beat the fromage frais with the vanilla essence and 4 teaspoons sugar. Spoon over the fruit. Cover and chill until required. When ready to serve, sprinkle the remaining sugar over the fromage frais. Place under a very hot grill until the sugar melts and turns golden brown. Serve immediately.

Fresh Fruit Compôte

125 kcals • serves 4

1 each of banana, orange, peach, apple, melon, pear	few drops of kirsh 1oz/30g demerara sugar

Prepare fruit: Slice banana, slice and core apple and pear and cut into eight. Remove rind and any pith from orange - divide into sections. Remove seeds from melon and cut into cubes. Remove stone from peach and cut into eight pieces. Mix all the fruit together, add Kirsh and sprinkle with sugar. Place in separate dishes, cover with tin foil and bake in oven 375°F, 190°C, Gas Mark 5 until soft.

Ice Cream

CHAMPNEYS

88 kcals per portion • Serves 4

10floz/330ml milk 1 vanilla pod, or a few drops of vanilla essence 1 teaspoon egg replacer	4 tablespoons low calorie, granulated sweetener 1 teaspoon cornflour, mixed with a little water to form a paste 2 teaspoons creme fraiche

Pour the milk into a saucepan, add the vanilla pod or essence and bring to the boil. Take a large bowl and lightly whip the egg replacer in 1 teaspoon of water. Add the sweetener and whisk until smooth. Put the cornflour into another large bowl. As soon as the milk comes to the boil, remove from the heat, discard the vanilla pod (if used) and pour the milk onto the paste, stirring continuously to thicken. Return the milk to the pan and simmer for 2 to 3 minutes to blend thoroughly, stirring from time to time. Pour the thickened milk onto the egg mixture, whisking with a fork while pouring. Leave until cool then fold in the creme fraiche. Pour the mixture through a fine sieve into a mixing bowl. Place in the freezer and whisk vigorously every 20 minutes with electric or rotary whisk until set (4 to 5 hours). The mixture can also be churned until firm in an ice cream machine. When set, place in a freezer container with an airtight lid.

Kiwi Cheesecake

220 kcals • Serves 6

4oz/115g digestive biscuit crumbs

3oz/85g butter, melted

2 teaspoons water

1 sachet low sugar lime jelly crystals

6fl oz/200ml boiling water

1 teaspoon castor sugar

8oz/225g carton low fat cottage cheese

3fl oz/105ml low fat plain yoghurt

Topping:

3 kiwi fruit, peeled and roughly chopped

few strands of orange peel

1fl oz/35ml pouring cream

1fl oz/35ml low fat plain yoghurt

Combine crumbs, butter and water, mixing well. Press mixture over 8in/20 cm loose bottom flan tin and refrigerate for 30 minutes. Make up jelly with the water, but keep from setting. Blend or process cottage cheese and yoghurt until smooth and add jelly, mixing well together. Pour filling over base and refrigerate until set. To make the topping, combine all the ingredients together and spread over the set filling. Decorate with slices of kiwi and thin strands of orange peel.

Lemon and Honey Syllabub with Strawberries

85 kcals per portion • Serves 4

1 lemon

3/4 pint/425ml fromage frais

1 tablespoon honey

1 egg white

3oz/85g strawberries, crushed

2 strawberries, halved

4 sprigs lemon balm

Remove the zest from the lemon and chop finely. Halve and squeeze the lemon and strain the juice. Whisk the egg white until stiff. Combine the fromage frais, lemon zest, juice and honey and gently fold in the egg white. Divide the crushed strawberries between the four dishes, fill with syllabub and decorate with half strawberries and sprigs of lemon balm.

Lemon and Orange Chiffon Pie

CHAMPNEYS

166 kcals • Serves 6

6oz/170g wholemeal flour	3 teaspoons arrowroot
2 tablespoons low-calorie, granulated sweetener	1oz/30g carob
3oz/85g polyunsaturated spread	8 egg whites
juice and zest of 6 oranges and 2 lemons	1 tablespoon raw cane sugar
	1 tablespoon clear honey

Preheat oven to 425°F, 220°C, Gas Mark 7. In a large mixing bowl rub together the flour, sweetener and polyunsaturated spread and bind with a little water. Roll out the dough on a lightly floured surface and use it to line a 10in/25cm flan ring and bake blind. Leave to cool. Cut the lemon and orange zest into fine strips and add to the lemon and orange juice. Bring to the boil in a small pan. Mix the arrowroot with a little water and add to the juices. Stir to thicken and remove the pan from the heat. When cool, chill in the fridge. Melt the carob and spread a thin layer inside the cooled pastry case and chill in the fridge. When set, pour in the orange and lemon mixture. Whisk together the egg whites, sugar and honey until the mixture forms peaks. Spread over the flan and lightly brown under a hot grill.

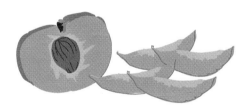

Nectarine Sorbet

FOREST MERE

250 kcals approximately • Serves 4

1 lb/450g ripe nectarines, stoned	1/4 pint/150ml water
4oz/115g sugar	juice of 1/2 lemon

Puree the fruit to a pulp. Boil the sugar and water together for 10 minutes and allow to cool slightly. Add the fruit and lemon juice to the cooled syrup. Stir well and transfer to a freezer tray or polythene container and freeze the until firm, stirring occasionally. This will take several hours. Store in the freezer until required. Bring to room temperature for about 10 minutes before serving.

Pineapple and Strawberry Strudel

75 kcals per portion • Serves 8

1 lb/450g strawberries, diced roughly	1 teaspoon ground cinnamon
1/2 pineapple, peeled and cut into cubes	8 leaves strudel pastry
2oz/55g fresh breadcrumbs	2 teaspoons vegetable oil

Mix together the strawberries, pineapple, breadcrumbs and cinnamon. Lay the strudel leaves on a towel, overlapping along the long side. Spread the filling along the entire length of the overlapping leaves, leaving 4in/10cm at each end. Using the towel as an aid, roll the strudel, tucking in the ends. Place on a baking sheet, using the towel to help lift the strudel. Brush with oil and bake for 30 minutes. Cool and serve sliced.

Plum and Orange Cobbler

SPRINGS HYDRO

332 kcals per portion • Serves 4

1 lb/450g Victoria plums, halved and stoned	1/2 teaspoon salt
3 large oranges	1oz/30g butter
2 tablespoons runny honey	1oz/30g light soft brown sugar
8oz/225g wholemeal flour	1/4 pint/150ml natural low fat yoghurt
2 teaspoons baking powder	1 tablespoon skimmed milk
1 teaspoon mixed spice	

Preheat the oven to 425°F, 220°C, Gas Mark 7. Halve and stone the plums. Place in a 2 pint/1 litre shallow oven proof dish with the juice of 2 oranges and the segments of the third orange. Drizzle the honey over the top. To make the scones, mix the flour, baking powder, spice and salt together on a bowl. Rub in the butter, then add the brown sugar and natural yoghurt. Knead together to form a soft dough. Roll the dough out on a lightly floured board to about 1/2 in/1cm thick, and cut out 8 x 2in/5cm rounds. Place on the fruit, overlapping around the dish. Lightly glaze with milk. Bake for 15 minutes or until the scones are brown and risen.

Raspberry Fool
STOBO CASTLE

This delectable summer dessert comes from Scotland,
where the raspberries are renowned for their quality and flavour.
It is easily prepared and low in calories.
60 kcals per portion • serves 4

8oz/225g fresh raspberries	1oz/30g gelatine
4 fl oz/115ml fresh orange juice	12 raspberries,
2 egg whites	and a few mint leaves to garnish
2oz/55g fromage frais	

Combine raspberries and orange juice in a liquidiser and sieve. Dissolve gelatine in a little of the puree over a very slow heat and add to raspberries. Whisk egg whites to a stiff peak and fold into the puree with the fromage frais. Pour into goblets and allow to set. Garnish with raspberries and mint.

Raspberry and Mango Flan
HOAR CROSS HALL
160 kcals per portion • Serves 8

4oz/115g margarine	2fl oz/70ml orange juice
8oz/225g wholemeal	6oz/170g low fat curd cheese
or stoneground flour	4fl oz/150ml milk
pinch of salt	8oz/225g raspberries
1 egg	mint leaves to garnish
1 mango	

Mix flour and salt and rub in the margarine until the mixture resembles breadcrumbs. Beat the egg and mix with enough water to make a soft dough. Leave for 30 minutes. Preheat the oven to 375°F, 190°C, Gas Mark 5. Roll out the pastry and use to line a small 6in/15cm flan dish. Cover the pastry base with tin foil and place some baking beans on the foil. Bake blind until the edges of the pastry are golden brown. Remove from the oven and leave to cool. Peel the mango and remove the stone. Liquidise the mango flesh with the orange juice. When the pastry has cooled pour the liquidised mango into the base. Liquidise 2oz/55g of the curd cheese with the milk to form a slightly thick sauce. Fill a piping bag fitted with a star nozzle with the rest of the curd cheese. Cover the mango mixture with raspberries and pipe the curd cheese onto the raspberries decoratively. Serve slices of flan sitting in a pool of cheese sauce garnished with mint.

Rhubarb Meringue

INGLEWOOD

24 kcals per portion • Serves 4

2 lb/910g rhubarb   low calorie sweetener

3 egg whites

Wash rhubarb and remove any strings. Cut into short pieces and stew in a small amount of water until soft. Put into an ovenproof dish and allow to cool. Add liquid sweetener to taste. Whip the egg whites until peaks form. Mix with enough sweetener to equal 1 tablespoon of sugar and pour this meringue over the rhubarb. Cook in a cool oven 275°F, 150°C, Gas Mark 1 for 2 hours until the meringue is firm. Serve immediately.

Special Pineapple Surprise

INGLEWOOD

168 kcals per portion • Serves 4

1 pineapple   4oz/115g grapes, de-seeded

1 orange, peeled and sliced   4floz/115ml sweet white wine

2 peaches, peeled and sliced   (1 wineglass)

Cut off the top of the pineapple just below the crown and trim the base of the fruit so it stands up straight. Wash the outside. Using a sharp knife, cut out the fruit of the pineapple in chunks and mix with the other fruit. Pour over the sweet white wine. Allow to stand and before serving pile the fruit back into the pineapple, replace the crown and place in a dish with the remainder of the fruit salad around it.

St Clements Mousse

HENLOW GRANGE

237 kcals per portion • Serves 4

4 eggs, separated ^{1}/$_2$oz/15g gelatine

4oz/115g soft brown sugar ^{1}/$_4$ pint/150ml natural low fat yoghurt

grated rind and juice 2 oranges   *To garnish:* finely shredded orange rind

grated rind and juice 2 lemons

Place the egg yolks, sugar, lemon and orange rind and orange juice in a bowl and whisk over a pan of barely simmering water until thick and mousse-like. Soak the gelatine in the lemon juice in a bowl. Place this bowl over a pan of simmering water and stir until dissolved. Fold into the mousse mixture together with the natural yoghurt. Whisk the egg whites until they form soft peaks. Carefully fold into the mousse. Divide the mixture between 4 individual dishes. Cover and chill until set. Serve, decorated with the orange rind.

Summer Pudding

210 kcals per portion • Serves 8

8oz/225g blackcurrants	4oz/1115g sugar
8oz/225g strawberries	1 pint/570ml orange juice
8oz/225g raspberries	12 slices white bread, crusts removed
8oz/225g blackberries	

Bring the fruit, orange juice and sugar to the boil then cool for 20 minutes. Line a 2lb/1kg pudding basin with bread, pour fruit mixture to one third full. Place a layer of bread and repeat twice more, finishing with a layer of bread. Ensure the bread is soaked well with juice. Leave to set for several hours, preferably overnight, before serving.

Wholemeal Pancake with a Fruit Filling

RAGDALE HALL

145 kcals per portion • Serves 5

4oz/115g wholemeal flour	5oz/140g cubed pineapple
1 beaten egg	3 skinned kiwi fruit
8fl oz/225ml skimmed milk	juice of 1 lime
pinch of salt	2 teaspoons low calorie sweetener
5oz/140g sliced strawberries	

Sift the flour and salt into bowl and mix in the egg and milk to make a pancake batter. Brush a small frying pan with sunflower oil (use a small pastry brush) and heat; use the batter to make 5 pancakes and leave to cool. Combine the pineapple and strawberries and divide equally between the pancakes, then fold each pancake in half. Blend the kiwi fruit, lime juice and sweetener and serve as a sauce with the pancakes.

Apple and Cheese Tea Bread
SHRUBLAND HALL

270 kcals per slice • Makes 1 large loaf (12 large slices)

4oz/115g very soft butter	3oz/85g Cheddar cheese, grated
4oz/115g sugar	1lb/450g cooking apples, peeled,
2 fresh eggs	cored and grated
10oz/285g self-raising flour	3oz/85g walnuts or pecan nuts, chopped
1/2 teaspoon salt	

Beat together butter, sugar and eggs until very light and fluffy. Sift dry ingredients together and fold into butter mixture. Mix in apples, cheese and nuts, blending quickly and thoroughly. Turn into a greased 1lb/450g loaf tin and bake in a medium oven 350°F, 180°C, Gas Mark 5 for about an hour until loaf is well risen and the top brown. Rest in tin for 5 minutes before turning out on rack to cool.

Apricot and Prune Loaf
SPRINGS HYDRO

142 kcals per slice • Makes 10 slices

2oz/55g dried apricots	1 teaspoon ground cinnamon
1 medium ripe banana	1 teaspoon ground ginger
8oz/225g wholemeal self raising flour	1 egg, beaten
1oz/30g caster sugar	3oz/85g non-soak dried prunes,
1oz/30g butter	stoned and chopped

Preheat the oven to 350°F, 180°C, Gas Mark 4. Lightly grease a 2lb/1kg loaf tin. Place the apricots in a small pan, add 1/4 pint/150ml water, bring to the boil and simmer for 5 minutes. Leave to cool. Blend together the apricots, water and banana until smooth in a blender. Place the flour and sugar in a large bowl, rub in the butter and add the spices. Beat in the egg and apricot and banana puree. Stir in the prunes. Pour into the prepared tin and bake for 45 minutes until firm. Cool slightly in the tin before turning out onto a wire rack.

Bacon and Herb Scones
RAGDALE HALL
165 kcals per scone • Makes 8 scones

8oz/225g finely milled wholemeal flour	2 teaspoons each of
2 teaspoons baking powder	parsley and chives, chopped
1/2 teaspoon mustard powder	6fl oz/170ml skimmed milk
4 rashers rindless smoked streaky bacon	8 tablespoons low fat cottage cheese
2oz/55g low fat spread	

Preheat oven to 350°F, 180°C, Gas Mark 4. Grill the bacon until crisp, cool and chop finely. Sift the flour and baking powder into a bowl and rub in the spread and mustard. Stir in bacon and herbs and enough milk to make a soft dough. Turn dough onto a floured surface and knead lightly. Roll out, cut into eight rounds and place on lightly greased baking tray. Brush the tops with milk and bake for about 15 minutes until golden. Serve warm with a tablespoon of low fat cottage cheese.

Carrot Cake
HENLOW GRANGE
490 kcals per average slice • Makes one large cake (12 slices)

10oz/285g soft light brown sugar	1 teaspoon mixed spice
8oz/225g butter	1 teaspoon ground ginger
grated rind of 1 orange	1 teaspoon ground nutmeg
4 eggs	1lb/450g carrots, peeled and finely grated
14oz/395g self raising flour	6oz/170g sultanas
2 teaspoons baking powder	4 -5 tablespoons milk or orange juice
1 teaspoon bicarbonate of soda	

Preheat oven to 350°F, 180°C, Gas Mark 4. Lightly grease and line a 10 inch/ 28cm round cake tin. In a large bowl cream together the sugar, butter and orange rind until light and fluffy. Gradually beat in the eggs with a little of the flour. Carefully fold in remaining flour and other dried ingredients and finally the grated carrot, sultanas, orange juice or milk. Transfer the mixture to the prepared tin and bake for just over 1 hour or until firm and slightly shrunken from the sides of the tin. Test with a skewer. Leave to cool in the tin before turning out.

Forest Mere Cake

FOREST MERE

Tiny wedges of this popular cake are served with afternoon tea at Forest Mere
220 kcals per small slice • Makes one large cake (20 small slices)

8oz/225g butter	2oz/55g ground almonds
8oz/225g demerara sugar	grated rind of I lemon
8oz/225g plain wholemeal flour	3 tablespoons milk
4 x size 2 eggs	8oz/115g sultanas
½ tablespoon baking powder	

Cream the butter and sugar until light and fluffy, then add eggs one at a time beating well after each. When the mixture is light and airy, add the ground almonds and grated lemon rind. Fold in the mixed flour and baking powder. Add the milk and mix thoroughly. Add the sultanas. (Do not beat once the fruit is added). Put into a lined 9in cake tin and bake for about I hour at 350°F, 180°C, Gas Mark 4. Cool in the tin before turning out.

Honey and Orange Bran Bread

SHRUBLAND HALL

Approximately 150 kcals per slice • Makes two loaves (10 slices per loaf)

I pint/570ml warm water	4oz/115g bran
2 tablespoons honey	1½ teaspoons salt
6 teaspoons dried yeast	2 tablespoons corn oil
1½ lb/680g brown bread flour	grated rind and juice of 2 oranges

Dissolve honey in warm water and sprinkle in the dried yeast. Leave until yeast is frothy (about 10 minutes). Add remaining ingredients and mix well. Knead until smooth. Divide in half and knead into 2 x 8in/20cm round cake tins sprinkled with flour and bran. Leave until loaves have risen to double original size. Bake for about 30 minutes in a hot oven 450°F, 230°C, Gas Mark 8. Turn out on rack to cool.

Index of Recipes

Also available from
DISCOVERY BOOKS

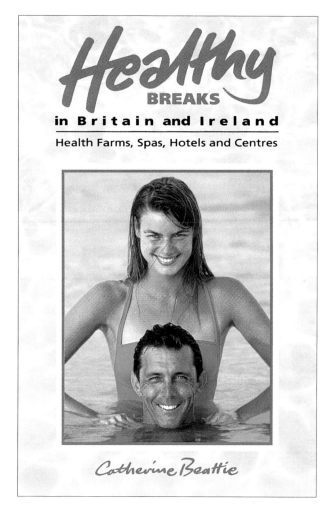

"All the information you need......"
Health & Fitness Magazine
"Packed with information"
Homes & Gardens

£9.99 from bookshops
or directly from Discovery Books
29 Hacketts Lane • Pyrford • Woking • Surrey • GU22 8PP
(please add £1.50 p&p)
Telephone 01932 346201